PEOPLES AND CULTURES OF AFRICA

SOUTHERN AFRICA

Edited by Peter Mitchell

CHELSEA HOUSE
PUBLISHERS
An imprint of Infobase Publishing

Chelsea House
An imprint of Infobase Publishing
132 West 31st Street
New York, NY 10001

Library of Congress Cataloging-in-Publication Data

Peoples and cultures of Africa / edited by Peter Mitchell.
    p. cm.
    "Authors, Amy-Jane Beer ... [et al.]"—T.p. verso.
    Includes bibliographical references and index.

    Set ISBN 0-8160-6260-9 (acid-free paper)

Nations & Personalities of Africa ISBN 0-8160-6266-8
Peoples and Cultures of Southern Africa ISBN 0-8160-6265-X
Peoples and Cultures of Central Africa ISBN 0-8160-6264-1
Peoples and Cultures of East Africa ISBN 0-8160-6263-3
Peoples and Cultures of West Africa ISBN 0-8160-6262-5
Peoples and Cultures of North Africa ISBN 0-8160-6261-7

    1. Africa—Civilization. 2. Ethnology—Africa. I. Beer, Amy-Jane. II. Mitchell, Peter, 1962-
    DT14.P46 2006
    960—dc22

                                    2006040011

For The Brown Reference Group plc.
Project Editor: Graham Bateman
Editors: Peter Lewis, Virginia Carter
Cartographers: Darren Awuah, Mark Walker
Designers: Steve McCurdy, Martin Anderson
Managing Editor: Bridget Giles
Production Director: Alastair Gourlay
Editorial Director: Lindsey Lowe

Consultant Editor

Dr. Peter Mitchell is University Lecturer in African Prehistory, and holds a Tutorial Fellowship in Archaeology at St. Hugh's College, University of Oxford, United Kingdom. He is also Curator of African Archaeology at the Pitt Rivers Museum, Oxford, and an academic member of the multidisciplinary African Studies Centre based at St. Antony's College, Oxford. He has previously worked at the University of Cape Town. He serves on the Governing Council of the British Institute in Eastern Africa and is a member of the editorial boards of numerous journals. From 2004–2006 he held the post of President of the Society of Africanist Archaeologists.

Advisory Editor

Dr. David Johnson is University Lecturer in Comparative and International Education (Developing Countries) and a Fellow of St. Antony's College, University of Oxford, United Kingdom. He is a member of the African Studies Centre, based at St. Antony's College, and has conducted research into education in a wide range of African countries. He serves on the United Kingdom National Commission for UNESCO's working committee on Africa and on the editorial boards of two international journals.

Authors
Chris Wingfield
with
Amy-Jane Beer
David Johnson
Peter Mitchell
Daniel Zimbler
Jarrad Zimbler

Title page *Skyscrapers in Johannesburg, South Africa.*

CONTENTS

Peoples and Cultures of Africa provides a region-based study of Africa's main ethnic groups, cultures, languages, religions, music, and much more. Five of the six volumes cover large geographical regions, namely: *North Africa, West Africa, East Africa, Central Africa,* and *Southern Africa*. Each of these volumes starts with a series of overview articles covering the political situation today, physical geography, biomes, peoples, cultures, and finally a historical time line. The main articles that follow are arranged A–Z with four types of articles, each distinguished by a characteristic running-head logo and color panel:

ETHNIC GROUPS, such as Maasai, Zulu, Yoruba. Each ethnic group article includes a Fact File and a map, giving the approximate area in which a people mainly live.

MATERIAL CULTURE, such as Contemporary Art, Metalwork, Sculpture, Textiles

PERFORMING ARTS AND LITERATURE, such as African-language Literature, Masks and Masquerade, Dance and Song

RELIGION, SOCIETY, AND CULTURE, such as Islam, Christianity, Marriage and the Family

The sixth volume (*Nations and Personalities*) is divided into three main sections: *Political and Physical Africa* presents a complete overview of Africa, followed by profiles of every nation on the continent; *International Organizations* and *Environmental Organizations* review major international bodies operating in the region; and *African Personalities* gives biographies of some 300 people from throughout Africa.

Within each volume there is a *Glossary* of key terms, lists of *Further Resources* such as other reference books, and useful Web sites. Volume *Indexes* are provided in volumes 1–5, with a complete *Set Index* in volume 6.

SOUTHERN AFRICA TODAY

SOUTHERN AFRICA PRESENTS A WIDE SPECTRUM OF THE WAYS IN WHICH PEOPLE LIVE, FROM THE GREAT WEALTH AND PRIVILEGE OF THE NORTHERN SUBURBS OF JOHANNESBURG IN SOUTH AFRICA TO THE HOE-FARMING LIFESTYLE AMONG THE RURAL PEOPLE OF SOUTHERN BOTSWANA, JUST HALF A DAY'S JOURNEY AWAY.

COUNTRY AND CITY

Although many of southern Africa's people still inhabit rural areas, living either by growing crops or by raising livestock or a combination of both, the region is rapidly becoming more urban. In South Africa, only 1.4 percent of the land area is occupied by Gauteng Province, which includes the large cities of Johannesburg and Pretoria, but around 20 percent of the country's population lives there. In contrast the Northern Cape Province makes up around 30 percent of the country, but contains just 1.8 percent of its people.

Much of the wealth and lure of Gauteng is associated with its gold mines. In 1980 South Africa was responsible for 70 percent of the world's gold production. Although gold production is now in decline, for more than a century from the 1880s on, migrant workers from rural communities all over southern Africa came to work in these mines, gaining a taste of urban life. In the course of that century South Africa came to dominate the other countries of the region in many ways.

SOUTH AFRICA'S DOMINANCE

In terms of both size and population, South Africa is by far the largest country in the region, with 44 million people, compared with population figures of around 19 million

A political map of southern Africa. Many of the countries in this region are rich in mineral resources, including gold, copper, diamonds, and uranium.

Affluence and poverty in South Africa. Alexandra township, inhabited by squatters, stands in sight of the wealthy Johannesburg suburb of Sandton City. The country's government is intent on building better housing for the majority of its citizens, who were disadvantaged by apartheid (1948–94).

for Mozambique, 13 million for Zimbabwe, 2 million for Namibia, 1.9 million for Lesotho, 1.6 million for Botswana, and 1.2 million for Swaziland (and 18 million for Madagascar). South Africa's borders are in many ways artificial colonial boundaries that cut across the historical territories of many of the peoples featured in this book.

South Africa also outstrips the rest of the region in its infrastructure and resources, with well-developed road and rail networks. It has many more towns than neighboring countries, which are dominated by their capital cities. South Africa, unusually, has three capitals: Cape Town, the legislative capital; Bloemfontein, the judicial capital; and Pretoria, the administrative capital (for which there is a proposed name change to Tshwane). Dealing with South Africa's economic and political dominance has been a challenge for other countries in the region.

BLACK-MAJORITY GOVERNMENT
Madagascar achieved its independence from France in 1960, while independence was granted to the former British protectorates of Botswana and Lesotho in 1966 and Swaziland in 1968. Bloody wars of liberation were followed by independence

and black-majority rule in Mozambique in 1975, Zimbabwe (formerly Rhodesia) in 1980, and Namibia in 1990.

In 1994, the world watched in admiration as peaceful elections brought an African National Congress (ANC) administration under its president Nelson Mandela (b.1918) to power in South Africa. After decades of apartheid—the segregation of the races with systematic discrimination against all non-whites—this was the country's first government to be elected with the participation of the large black majority, who make up 80 percent of the population. At that time, South Africa was the last African country to be controlled by a white minority (comprising 10 percent of the population). However, just 35 years earlier, all of the countries in southern Africa had been in this position.

A NEW ERA
Southern African politics are still in a state of great upheaval. The time of transition has not been eased by the specter of AIDS and an HIV infection rate of 30–40 percent across the region. In addition, the controversial question of land reform dominates politics in Zimbabwe. Most people there and in neighboring countries agree that land needs to be redistributed more fairly to right the injustices of colonialism. Yet President Robert Mugabe's seizure of farms and intimidation of political opponents have crippled the country's economy and created food shortages.

THE MAIN PHYSICAL FEATURE OF SOUTHERN AFRICA IS ITS DRY INTERIOR PLATEAU, WHICH LIES AT AN ELEVATION OF 3,280–6,500 FEET (1,000–2,000 M). THIS PLATEAU IS CROSSED BY A NUMBER OF MAJOR RIVERS, WHICH HAVE IN THE PAST FORMED BOTH BOUNDARIES AND TRADE AND MIGRATION ROUTES. DESERTS CHARACTERIZE SOUTHERN AFRICA'S WEST COAST, WHILE THE WETTER EAST IS MORE FERTILE AND SO MORE HEAVILY POPULATED.

RIVERS

Rivers mark many of the boundaries between modern states in southern Africa. They were used as frontiers by European settlers to demarcate the areas under their control. These were formalized by the end of the 19th century.

Southern Africa is the region that lies south of the Zambezi and Cunene rivers, which form part of the northern borders of Namibia and Zimbabwe. The Zambezi cuts across Mozambique, and was an important avenue of trade for the Portuguese in the colonial period. Madagascar and the Comoro Islands are included in this section, but could as easily be grouped with East Africa.

Other rivers that are important boundary markers include the Limpopo, which forms the northern boundary of South Africa, the Molopo, an often dry river that defines the southern border of Botswana, and the Caledon, which forms the western border of Lesotho. The Gariep (formerly Orange) forms the southern boundary of Namibia with South Africa; this river once formed the northern frontier of the Cape Colony.

In the southeast of the region, the limits of European settlement were also defined by large rivers. Initially, the frontier was at the Great Fish River, before being pushed north to the Great Kei River. Later still, the Thukela River formed an effective boundary between the British in Natal and the Zulu nation. Many historic and contemporary places, such as Transvaal, Orange Free State, and Transkei, are named for rivers.

LAKES AND DAMS

The general shortage of water throughout the region has led to the creation of a number of large artificial lakes and dams to supply people's needs. Lake Kariba and Lake

Victoria Falls on the Middle Zambezi River, on the Zimbabwe–Zambia frontier are 355 feet (108 m) high. They were named for Queen Victoria of Great Britain by the explorer David Livingstone in 1856.

Map of southern Africa showing the main physical features of the region. The landscape here varies enormously, from mountains to deserts to the wildlife-rich swamps of the Okavango delta.

Table Mountain near Cape Town, South Africa. The dense, white cloud that often forms on top of this flat-topped mountain is known as the "tablecloth."

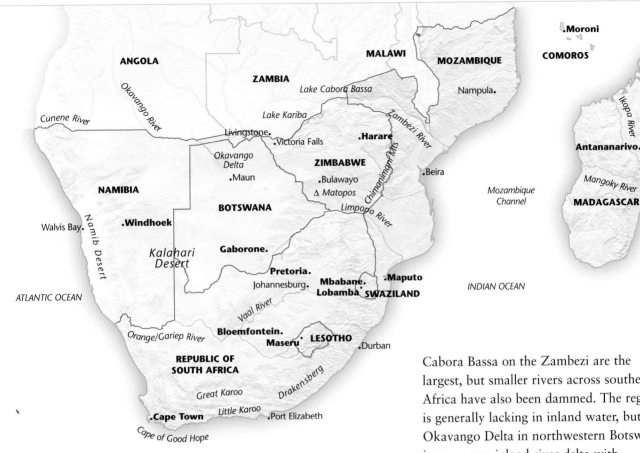

ANGOLA

ZAMBIA

Cunene River

Okavango River

MALAWI

Lake Cabora Bassa

Lake Kariba

Livingstone.

.Victoria Falls

Zambezi River

MOZAMBIQUE

Nampula.

.Moroni

COMOROS

Ikopa River

.Harare

ZIMBABWE

.Bulawayo

Δ Matopos

Okavango Delta

.Maun

NAMIBIA

Namib Desert

Walvis Bay.

.Windhoek

Kalahari Desert

BOTSWANA

Gaborone.

Chimanimani Mts

.Beira

Limpopo River

Antananarivo.

Mangoky River

MADAGASCAR

Mozambique Channel

ATLANTIC OCEAN

Pretoria.

Johannesburg.

Vaal River

Mbabane.

Lobamba

.Maputo

SWAZILAND

INDIAN OCEAN

Orange/Gariep River

Bloemfontein.

Maseru.

LESOTHO

.Durban

REPUBLIC OF
SOUTH AFRICA

Great Karoo

Drakensberg

.Cape Town

Little Karoo

.Port Elizabeth

Cape of Good Hope

Cabora Bassa on the Zambezi are the largest, but smaller rivers across southern Africa have also been dammed. The region is generally lacking in inland water, but the Okavango Delta in northwestern Botswana is a swampy inland river delta with abundant wildlife, which has developed at the point where the Cubango River spreads out as it drains into the northern sands of the Kalahari Desert.

MOUNTAINS AND COAST

Except for a few hilly outcrops, such as the Matopos in Zimbabwe, the interior plateau of southern Africa is largely flat. A string of mountains marks the drop in altitude to the low coastal plain. The Cape Fold Mountains extend into the Drakensberg ranges, which stretch all the way up to the Chimanimani mountains in the east of Zimbabwe. The land between these mountains and the coast receives more rain and forms a lush coastal plain. By contrast, the western part of the high interior plateau—the Great Karoo—is a semiarid scrubland region. Farther west, the land becomes progressively drier. The west coast bordering the Atlantic Ocean north of the Cape of Good Hope sees very little rainfall, and becomes the waterless Namib Desert beyond the Gariep River.

SOUTHERN AFRICA'S CLIMATE IS LARGELY WARM TEMPERATE. THE REGION'S ECOLOGICAL ZONES OR BIOMES ARE DEFINED BY RAINFALL AND ALTITUDE. THE FARTHER WEST ONE GOES, THE DRIER THE LANDSCAPE BECOMES; THE NAMIB DESERT IS ONE OF THE DRIEST PLACES ON EARTH. IN THE EAST, RAIN IS PLENTIFUL AND THE SUN'S WARMTH IS TEMPERED BY ALTITUDE IN THE DRAKENSBERG MOUNTAINS, WHERE WINTER FROSTS OCCUR.

A crowned lemur (Eulemur cornatus) from northern Madagascar. Lemurs are found only on this large island. There are more than 35 species, but many are threatened by the loss of their habitat.

DESERT/XERIC SCRUB: KAROO, KALAHARI, NAMIB

The arid areas of southern Africa range from the dry (xeric) scrub typified by the South African Karoo, through the sparsely vegetated and largely stony Kalahari Desert to the epic dune landscape of the northern Namib Desert. The Karoo is vegetated with drought-resistant grasses, dotted with succulent, water-storing plants, and home to brown hyenas, springhares, black storks, and, in summer, European swifts. The Namib is among the driest deserts in the world, yet even here, some plants survive, like the extraordinary "living stones" (*Lithops* spp.) and the bizarre welwitschia, with its single spear of ever-growing leaves. Both gain almost all the water they need to survive from sea fogs that roll in from Namibia's Skeleton Coast.

MEDITERRANEAN SCRUB: FYNBOS

The southwestern corner of South Africa comprises a unique biome. It vaguely resembles the biome that exists on the shores of the faraway Mediterranean Sea, but its flora is quite unlike that found anywhere else. The region receives moderate rainfall in winter but is regularly burned by fast-moving bushfires during the long, dry summers. Many of the region's native plants, including the spectacular proteas, are fire-adapted—their seeds cannot germinate without fire.

MONTANE GRASSLAND: VELDT

Much of the eastern half of southern Africa is uplands, which receive more rainfall than the plains farther west. Plant life there reflects a slightly cooler, wetter climate. The grassy, rolling terrain of the Drakensberg and Maloti plateaus is known as the highveld (*veld* is

1

2

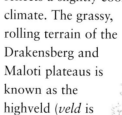

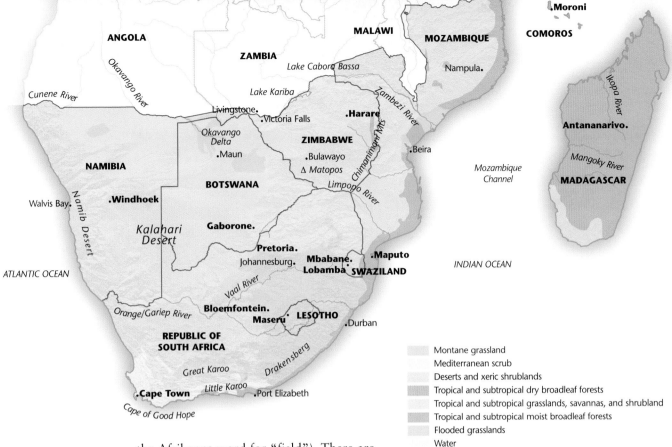

Map legend:
- Montane grassland
- Mediterranean scrub
- Deserts and xeric shrublands
- Tropical and subtropical dry broadleaf forests
- Tropical and subtropical grasslands, savannas, and shrubland
- Tropical and subtropical moist broadleaf forests
- Flooded grasslands
- Water

the Afrikaans word for "field"). There are relatively few trees. Most of the region is given over to agriculture, and the remaining areas of natural grassland and heath are home to limited wildlife.

TROPICAL GRASSLAND/SAVANNA: SOUTHERN AFRICAN PLAINS

The vast savanna of southern Africa is a continuation of that in East Africa, from which it is separated by the southern Rift Zone. Biologically, these twin zones of grassland and scrub have much in common, in particular fast-growing grasses support huge herds of large herbivores, which in turn feed large carnivores. The area supports the classic African "safari" animals—lions, cheetahs, zebra, wildebeest, rhinos, and African wild dogs. To the east, the savanna merges with the highveld in a region of scrubby open woodland, the bushveld.

SUBTROPICAL BROADLEAF AND MIXED FOREST: EAST COAST FORESTS

The eastern and southeastern coasts of southern Africa receive more rainfall than other parts of the region—enough to support a ribbon of mixed forest. In places

these forests grow rooted in beach sand, right down to the high tide mark. The coast zone also boasts a mosaic of grassland, swamps and wetland and so biodiversity is high, especially for birds and invertebrates, though large mammals are less common.

MADAGASCAR, A LAND APART

The great island of Madagascar is ecologically so distinct that it almost qualifies as a mini-continent in its own right. Like the mainland, its east coast experiences high rainfall, and supports dense, humid forest, while the west coast is drier, with several unique variations on the dry broadleaf forest biome—mainly thorn thickets and woodlands. Because Madagascar has been isolated from the mainland for 150 million years, the island has a highly distinct fauna (all the animals in a region). About one in ten land-dwelling species here are found nowhere else, earning Madagascar the nickname "nature's laboratory." These species include several chameleons and tortoises, some unusual carnivores like the fossa, and a whole branch of the primate family tree, the lemurs.

Animal species of southern Africa:
1 *White rhinoceros* (Ceratotherium simum);
2 *Lion* (Panthera leo);
3 *Springbok* (Antidorcas marsupialis); 4 *Meerkat* (Suricata suricatta).

THE GREATEST DIVERSITY IN SOUTHERN AFRICA EXISTS AMONG THE PEOPLE WHO LIVE THERE. AT THE SOUTHERN END OF THE VAST CONTINENT, THE REGION HAS FOR THOUSANDS OF YEARS BEEN THE DESTINATION FOR MIGRATIONS OF PEOPLES FROM FARTHER NORTH, WHICH ADDED TO THE EXISTING DIVERSITY OF THE INDIGENOUS GROUPS.

KHOISAN LANGUAGE FAMILY

RELIGION

Some 80 percent of southern Africans identify themselves as Christians, including around one-quarter of the Asian population. While Dutch Reformed Church membership is especially strong among the Afrikaans-speaking Afrikaner and "Cape Coloured" communities, Zionist, Apostolic, and Independent churches have many adherents among Bantu speakers. The Methodist, Catholic, and Anglican churches also have a strong following in southern Africa.

The next most widely practiced of the world religions is Islam. Around 25 percent of the Asian community, along with most Cape Malays, are Muslim. However, Islam still only accounts for around 1 percent of the entire population of southern Africa.

Around half of southern Africa's Asian population—totaling just under 600,000 people and concentrated mainly on Durban in KwaZulu–Natal province—are Hindu. There are also some 80,000 Jewish people resident in southern Africa, mainly in the cities of Cape Town and Johannesburg.

Many southern Africans mix preexisting religious practices, such as the veneration of ancestors, with their Christianity. Showing respects to ancestors is part of everyday life, and people do not necessarily see such observances as distinct aspects of a religion.

LANGUAGES

There are three main groups of languages spoken in southern Africa: Khoisan, Bantu, and Germanic languages.

Khoisan Languages

This language family, which includes the languages spoken by the region's earliest known inhabitants, originated in southern Africa. It can be divided into three main groups: northern, central, and southern Khoisan. The central group includes the languages spoken by Khoikhoi peoples of the past, as well as Nama, which has around 150,000 speakers, plus a number of San languages. Altogether, Khoisan languages are now spoken by only some 250,000 people. The Khoisan languages are often referred to as "click" languages because of their distinctive use of clicks or popping sounds.

Bantu Languages

These languages likely originated centuries ago in the forested regions of west-central Africa to the north. Today, Bantu speakers live throughout West, Central, and East Africa. In southern Africa Bantu languages may by divided into two major categories:, the Southern and Southwestern groups.

Southern Bantu languages constitute the major group, and include the following:

Above and opposite: Summary family trees of the Khoisan and Niger-Congo language groups. The ethnic groups featured in this volume are listed in parentheses after the relevant language.

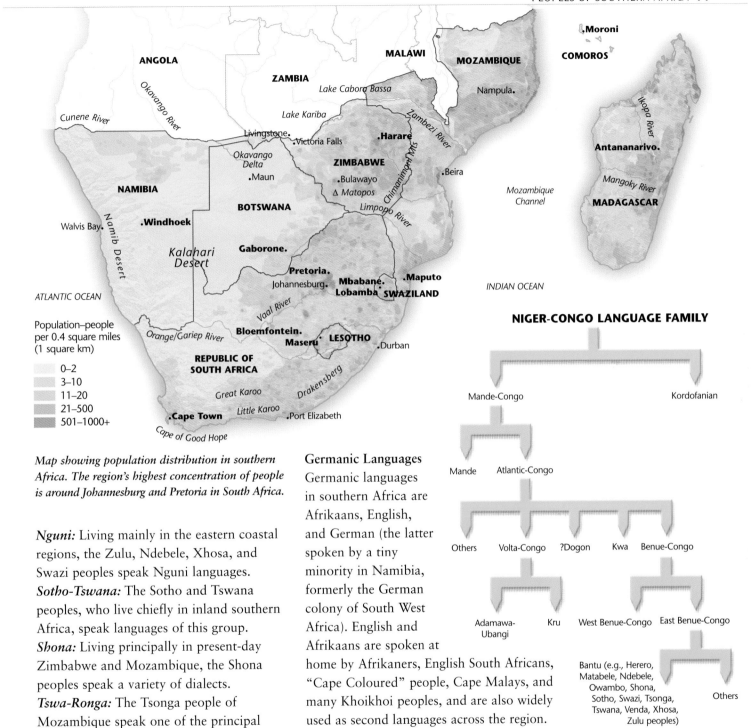

Map showing population distribution in southern Africa. The region's highest concentration of people is around Johannesburg and Pretoria in South Africa.

Nguni: Living mainly in the eastern coastal regions, the Zulu, Ndebele, Xhosa, and Swazi peoples speak Nguni languages.

Sotho-Tswana: The Sotho and Tswana peoples, who live chiefly in inland southern Africa, speak languages of this group.

Shona: Living principally in present-day Zimbabwe and Mozambique, the Shona peoples speak a variety of dialects.

Tswa-Ronga: The Tsonga people of Mozambique speak one of the principal languages of this group.

Venda: The language spoken by Venda people is in a class of its own, although it has similarities to both its neighbors, the Shona and Sotho–Tswana groups.

The languages of the Owambo and Herero peoples of Namibia are also Bantu languages, but belong to the Southwestern group, which has more in common with languages spoken in Angola.

Germanic Languages

Germanic languages in southern Africa are Afrikaans, English, and German (the latter spoken by a tiny minority in Namibia, formerly the German colony of South West Africa). English and Afrikaans are spoken at home by Afrikaners, English South Africans, "Cape Coloured" people, Cape Malays, and many Khoikhoi peoples, and are also widely used as second languages across the region.

Other Languages

Other languages include Hindi and Urdu; however, in a census in the early 2000s, 90 percent of South African Asians said that they spoke English at home.

Malagasy, which is spoken by some 18 million people on the island of Madagascar, has much in common with the languages of Indonesia and Malaysia.

RELIGION, LANGUAGE, ETHNICITY, MATERIAL AND ARTISTIC TRADITIONS, AND SOCIAL STRUCTURES AND NORMS, AS WELL AS INDIVIDUAL CHOICE, ARE THE MAIN DEFINING ASPECTS OF CULTURES. SOUTHERN AFRICA, WITH ITS MULTITUDE OF LANGUAGES, ETHNICITIES, AND ARTISTIC FORMS, HAS A COMPLEX AND EVOLVING CULTURAL MAP.

ARTS AND CRAFTS

Western traditions differentiate between arts, which are aesthetic objects created "for art's sake" and crafts, which are pleasing objects designed to perform some useful function. Yet this distinction is increasingly unclear in the West, and it can rarely be applied to Africa's artistic traditions, which make no such distinction.

Many of southern Africa's arts have their roots firmly in village-based ways of life, involving the decoration of utensils, clothing, houses, and the human body. As artists respond to political and economic changes, some artisans have become full-time professionals. Zulu baskets, San ostrich eggshell beads, and Himba jewelry were all originally made for day-to-day use. Today, artisans often create items to sell to the growing tourist market. Zulu, Xhosa, and Ndebele beadwork was originally made into body ornaments, but has become so popular that today it is possible to buy all kinds of beaded objects, such as mugs and salt cellars.

New traditions have also grown up. Zulu baskets made from telephone wire have become widely popular, as have Shona stone carvings and San paintings.

Some artists have achieved international fame, such as the Ndzundza Ndebele house mural painter Esther Mahlangu (b.1935). Her

A Tswana woman weaving a basket. The various patterns are passed from generation to generation and are associated with the Tswana people's culture.

fellow South African Willie Bester (b.1956) has built on township traditions of working with discarded and recycled materials to create controversial metal sculptures.

MUSIC AND DANCE

Music and dance are key parts of many ceremonies, such as the San trance dance, Sotho, Tswana, and Venda initiations, and the Swazi "first-fruits" ceremony. The introduction of competitions for migrant workers at the region's mines stimulated new forms of music and dance. For example, *isicathamiya*, a style of unaccompanied singing in close harmony performed most famously by the Zulu group Ladysmith Black Mambazo, developed there, as did gumboot dancing, a rhythmic, stamping dance using miners' boots.

For the "Cape Coloured" community, the Cape Town Minstrel Carnival is a major dance and music event celebrating the end of slavery. This Dixieland-inspired festival and other American musical forms, such as swing and jive, combined with local styles to create township jazz. The jazz pianist Abdullah Ibrahim (formerly Dollar Brand; b.1934), who comes from the Cape Coloured community, became internationally famous, along with his fellow South African musicians, the trumpeter Hugh Masekela (b.1939) and the singer Miriam Makeba (b.1932). Other artists who have achieved international recognition are the South African reggae singer Lucky Dube (b.1964) and the Zimbabwean Thomas Mapfumo (b.1945), who plays music based on the Shona mbira, or thumb piano.

From the 1970s on, African American music continued to influence southern African artists, who interpreted and adapted it and created an original pop music scene, especially in South Africa. The "bubblegum" pop music of the flamboyant singer Brenda Fassi reinterpreted the power pop of Tina Turner for African audiences. *Kwaito* developed as a distinct regional form of hip-hop in the 1990s.

STORYTELLING

Most southern African peoples have a long history of storytelling, often called oral literature, since it embraces various forms such as parables, poetry, epic poems, fables, myths and legends and is passed down from generation to generation by word of mouth, often in song. Oral literature also includes the histories of famous people, clans, and kingdoms. For this reason, oral literature is also known as oral history. Widespread education has allowed these traditions to

The Chopi people of Mozambique often use their characteristic timbila xylophones to accompany lively song and dance performances reflecting and commenting on village history.

feed into written forms such as novels, short stories, poetry, and plays, which are published in English, Portuguese, Afrikaans, and an increasing number of African languages. Storytelling is also making the leap into new forms of popular media such as movies, radio, and television. Soap operas in particular are having a huge impact through telling stories that relate to the aspirations and possibilities of the new political situation in southern Africa.

CHOPI

The Chopi are a subgroup of the Tsonga people who live mainly in the coastal Inhambane region of Mozambique. In particular, they are well known for their music, which features a unique type of xylophone known as a *mbila* (plural, *timbila*). This instrument is of Southeast Asian origin and is thought to have been introduced to the area either directly from Indonesia or via Madagascar. Many complex compositions have been written for *timbila* ensembles, which generally involve an orchestra of around ten xylophones of four different sizes. Famous *timbila* performers include Eduardo Durão and Venancio Mbande.

3 million years ago Early hominids present in southern Africa.

100,000 years ago First modern humans present.

27,000 years ago Earliest known rock paintings created, in present-day Namibia.

20,000 years ago Later Stone Age culture similar to that of the San established across southern Africa.

2000 years ago Earliest use of domestic animals in the world, in southern Africa, may suggest the development of a Khoikhoi lifestyle.

1500 years ago Evidence of iron, food-production, and particular pottery styles in the archaeological record suggests the arrival of Bantu-speaking peoples.

650–1300 c.e. Large cattle-owning Toutswe communities exist (in Botswana).

800–1200 Emergence of a hierarchical society in the Limpopo valley, peaking in southern Africa's first state at the site of Mapungubwe (c.1220–1300).

1000 Nguni-speaking people settle the eastern seaboard of South Africa, with Sotho–Tswana-speakers arriving a few centuries later.

1000s Bantu-speaking peoples migrate from East Africa to Madagascar.

1220–1300 Mapungubwe trading center at the height of its prosperity.

1290 Great Zimbabwe becomes capital of a major kingdom trading gold across the Indian Ocean.

c.1450 The site at Great Zimbabwe is abandoned; Mutota becomes the first leader (*mwene mutapa*) of the Shona Mutapa state in northeastern Zimbabwe.

1480s Kingdom of Mutapa breaks up after death of second ruler Matope; southern part of kingdom comes under control of the Rozwi, a Shona subgroup.

1488 Portuguese navigator Bartolomeu Dias and his crew are the first Europeans to round the Cape of Good Hope (which Dias names the "Cape of Storms").

1500s–1700s Tsonga kingdoms (Nyaka, Tembe, and Maputo) flourish successively in Mozambique.

1505 Portuguese port established at Sofala in Mozambique to trade beads and cloth for gold and ivory with the Shona.

1650–80 The Pedi (northern Sotho) state established in northern South Africa.

1652 Jan van Riebeeck founds a fort and provisioning station at Table Bay for the Dutch East India Company. In 1658 slaves are brought there from Indonesia and Malaysia. When van Riebeeck leaves the Cape in 1662, slaves outnumber free people there. The local Khoikhoi, alarmed at the permanent Dutch presence, try to expel them in 1659. This is followed by further wars between 1673 and 1677.

Ship's doctor Jan van Riebeeck began Dutch colonization in South Africa when he founded a settlement at the Cape.

c.1684 Rozwi state founded (in modern Zimbabwe and parts of modern Botswana and Transvaal) by Changamire Dombo I; Rozwi expel Portuguese from the Zambezi valley in the 1690s.

1688 150 French Protestants, or Huguenots, arrive in the Cape and Trekboers (pioneer farmers) begin to move inland away from Company control.

The hill complex at Great Zimbabwe. A thriving Shona culture was based at this ancient granite-walled site, reaching its peak in the 1300s and 1400s. Its inhabitants lived from farming, mining, and trade—the settlement was ideally situated to control trade routes between the interior and the ports on the east coast.

1713   Smallpox epidemic in the Cape kills many Khoikhoi.

1779   First of nine frontier wars with the Xhosa sees the Great Fish River established as a frontier of white settlement.

1783–1810 Reign of King Andrianampoinimerina, founder of the Merina kingdom on Madagascar.

1795–1803 The British take Cape Town to prevent it falling into French hands.

1804   Ancestors of the Griqua, calling themselves the "Basters," cross the Orange (Gariep) river, leaving the Cape Colony behind.

1806   British invade the Cape again and take formal control in 1814; by this time the colony is made up of 20,000 white settlers, 15,000 Khoisan, and 25,000 slaves of various origins.

1816   Zulu Chief Senzagakona dies and his third son Shaka is released from the military service of Mthethwa king Dingiswayo to take over the small Zulu chieftancy.

1816–19 Wars between the Nguni kingdoms of Ngwane, Ndwandwe, and Mthethwa in eastern southern Africa. The Mthethwa kingdom is destroyed by the Ndwandwe in 1818 and King Dingiswayo is killed.

1818–19 Shaka reorganizes the Mthethwa chiefdoms and army, bringing them under Zulu control; the Zulu conquer the Ndwandwe.

c.1819–c.1839 Shaka and his Zulu kingdom rise to power along the coast, causing mass migrations and wars across the eastern region; this period is called the Mfecane (crushing) by Nguni peoples, and the Difaqane (scattering) by Sotho–Tswana peoples.

1820   British settlers housed along frontier with Xhosa, having been promised fertile land.

1820–21 Invasion of Nguni from Zululand in Mozambique, conquering the Tsonga.

1822   Mzilikazi moves away from Shaka into interior of South Africa. He overcomes the Pedi state in 1826 and founds the Ndebele kingdom.

1824   Moshoeshoe, a Sotho leader, offers refuge to people fleeing the Mfecane and founds the Basuto kingdom.

1828   Zulu King Shaka is killed by his brother Dingaan.

1833   Act of Parliament banning slavery across the British empire sees the emancipation of slaves between 1834 and 1838.

King Shaka of the Zulu (c.1787–1828) was a brilliant military commander. From 1816, he reorganized his people into a formidable nation that quickly became the most powerful state in southern Africa. Other African peoples, Afrikaners, and the British all came to fear and respect the Zulus' fighting prowess.

1835   Voortrekkers (Afrikaner pioneers) cross the Orange river into areas devastated by the Mfecane, where they found the Transvaal and Orange Free State. South of Zululand they create the Republic of Natalia.

1837   The Voortrekkers force Mzilikazi to cross the Limpopo river, where his people take the name Matabele.

1838   Boers stage a revenge attack on the Zulu, killing some 3,000 at the Battle of Blood River.

1840s–1880s Wars between the Nama and Herero in Namibia.

1843   British annex Natalia as the Crown Colony of Natal.

1843 The Griqua under their leader Adam Kok III form an alliance with the British.

1846–47 The War of the Ax sees Xhosa territory between the Keiskama and Kei rivers annexed as "British Kaffraria." In 1865 it becomes part of the Cape Colony.

1849–52 Crown Colony of Natal colonized by British settlers. Indentured laborers from India are also brought here after 1860.

1857 Famine among the Xhosa follows a prophecy that if all cattle and crops are destroyed, the whites will be driven into the sea.

1860–67 Venda and Sotho drive Boers out from lands north of the Olifants river.

1861 Trek to found Griqualand East is led by Adam Kok III with the encouragement of the British.

1865 A census of the Cape Colony shows 181,592 Europeans, 81,598 Khoikhoi, 100,536 black people, and 132,655 others.

1867 Discovery of diamonds near Kimberley results in a sudden influx of immigrants and the area (Griqualand West) being annexed by Britain in 1871.

The mine workings at Kimberley shortly after diamonds were discovered there in 1867. The Griqua who lived in the area were forced out as different groups of white settlers disputed control.

1868 Moshoeshoe asks the British for protection, who annex Basutoland (Lesotho). Moshoeshoe dies in 1870 with his nation numbering 150,000 people. The British transfer control of Basutoland to the Cape Colony.

1877–81 The discovery of gold in the Transvaal brings an expansion of British control; the Namibian port of Walvis Bay is annexed in 1878, and Griqualand East and the Transvaal in 1879. 1879 also witnesses an Anglo-Zulu war; British forces suffer a major defeat at the Battle of Isandhlwana before overcoming the Zulu.

1881 First Anglo-Boer War; the Boers defeat the British at the Battle of Majuba, while the Gun War between the Basotho and the Cape Colony sees Basutoland revert to direct rule from Britain.

1884 Germans occupy South West Africa (now Namibia).

1885 Tswana lobby for British protection and lands south of Molopo river become Crown Colony of Bechuanaland, while those to the north become the British protectorate of Bechuanaland.

The heroic defense of the border post at Rorke's Drift during the Anglo-Zulu War of 1879 is famed in British military history. It helped boost morale after Britain's crushing defeat at Isandhlwana. Eventually, British military might prevailed and King Cetshwayo's Zulu kingdom was occupied and split up.

1887 Zululand annexed by Britain and later incorporated into the Colony of Natal.

1888 Matabele King Lobengula, son of Mzilikazi, is persuaded to give mining rights to the British South African Company (BSAC), controlled by Cecil Rhodes. A year later the BSAC is given a charter to govern the Bechuanaland protectorate (Botswana). In 1890 it invades Shona lands, and in 1891 the borders of Mozambique are defined with Portugal. In 1893 the Matabele are also conquered by the BSAC.

1895 Crown Colony of Bechuanaland becomes part of the Cape Colony, while the British protectorate of Bechuanaland is removed from BSAC control after a petition from Tswana leaders.

1896 French conquer Madagascar.

1896–98 In Zimbabwe the first *chimurenga* (uprising) against BSAC rule unites the Shona and Matabele peoples.

1899–1902 Second Anglo-Boer War ends in a Boer defeat and the Afrikaner republics of the Transvaal and Orange Free State become British colonies. Swaziland becomes a British protectorate.

1904 Herero and Nama resistance against the Germans in Namibia sees many killed and their land confiscated.

1910 The Union of South Africa unites the former Boer republics with the British Natal and Cape colonies.

1912 South African Native National Congress (SANNC) is established; main goal is to maintain voting rights for "Coloureds" (an official term for people of mixed heritage) and black Africans in Cape Province.

1913 Native Land Act denies black South Africans the right to buy or rent land outside of their designated "native reserves." More than 60 percent of the population is restricted to less than 8 percent of South Africa's land. Many people starve on the reserves.

1914 Outbreak of World War I between Britain and Germany incites the last major Boer rebellion. German South West Africa taken by a combination of South African and Portuguese forces. Control of the area transferred to South Africa after the war.

1923 SANNC renamed the African National Congress (ANC) to reflect its broad goal of winning voting rights for all South Africans.

1925 Afrikaans replaces Dutch as an official language in South Africa.

1933 D. F. Malan forms the Purified National Party in South Africa.

1939–45 During World War II, troops across the region are committed to the Allied cause.

1948 Afrikaner National Party comes to power in South Africa promising to send all black people to reserves (later called "homelands"), run a white-only economy, and enshrine in law the racist policies of apartheid, an Afrikaans word meaning "separate development." Every person is classified by race. People's race determines where they can live, work, and whom they may marry (interracial marriages are illegal). The best jobs and land are reserved for whites while the rights of black people are increasingly restricted or taken away, including the right to vote.

The Second Anglo-Boer War of 1899–1902 was the outcome of a long struggle for supremacy in South Africa between Dutch and English settlers. To defeat the guerrilla tactics of the tenacious Boers, the British interned their families in concentration camps.

1955   In South Africa, the Bantu Education Act grants a very poor quality education to black students, preparing them for the roles of domestic servants and laborers.

1958   Establishment of Owamboland People's Congress, which in 1960 becomes SWAPO, the South West Africa People's Organization.

1959   South Africa's native reserves are reorganized into Bantustans; eventually, over 3 million black people are evicted from "white" areas to these "homelands."

1960   British Prime Minister Harold Macmillan, visiting Cape Town, heralds African nationalism as an unstoppable "wind of change." Sharpeville massacre: 69 demonstrators for the newly formed Pan-African Congress are shot dead by South African police, mostly in the back. ANC is banned in South Africa.

1961   South Africa becomes a republic after a referendum and the ANC launches armed resistance to apartheid rule. In Southern Rhodesia the Zimbabwe African People's Union (ZAPU) is formed under leader Joshua Nkomo to oppose continued white-settler rule.

1962   ANC leader Nelson Mandela arrested, tried for conspiracy at the Rivonia Trial of 1963, and sentenced to life imprisonment on Robben Island in 1964.

1965   Unilateral Declaration of Independence (UDI) from Britain by white Southern Rhodesian leader Ian Smith leads to guerrilla warfare in country (which changes its name to Rhodesia) and international sanctions.

1966   Independence granted to the British protectorates of Botswana and Lesotho. U.N. General Assembly votes to terminate South Africa's mandate in Namibia, but this is ignored, resulting in guerrilla war by SWAPO.

1968   Swaziland granted independence.

1974–75   Military coup in Portugal brings rapid decolonization of Mozambique and Angola. Independent People's Republic of Mozambique proclaimed with Frelimo's leader Samora Machel as president. The South African-backed Renamo movement fights against Frelimo, bringing 17 more years of war to Mozambique. South Africa also intervenes militarily against the Cuban-backed government of Angola.

1976   700 people die in major nationwide anti-apartheid riots in South Africa. They are sparked by a strike of school students in Soweto township, Johannesburg, protesting a new ruling that they must be taught in Afrikaans.

1977   Steve Biko, popular leader of the South African black consciousness movement, is killed in police custody.

1979   Settlement brokered by Britain (Lancaster House agreement) between illegal UDI regime in Rhodesia and nationalist insurgents; white rule ends and the country wins independence as Zimbabwe.

1980   First multiracial Zimbabwean elections won by ZANU under Robert Mugabe.

1983   In South Africa those classifed by apartheid as "Coloureds" and Indians are given limited voting rights and representation in government.

1983–84   Following clashes between (mostly Shona) supporters of the ZANU government of Zimbabwe and (mostly Matabele) followers of Joshua Nkomo's ZAPU in Matabeleland, the North Korean-trained Fifth Brigade of the Zimbabwean Army is sent to pacify the region, resulting in thousands of civilian deaths.

1985   State of emergency declared in South Africa.

1986–95   Violent conflict between supporters of the ANC and the Zulu Inkatha Freedom Party in KwaZulu and the Witwatersrand mining area around Johannesburg.

1988   Deal struck for the removal of Cuban troops from Angola in return for Namibian independence. UN-supervised elections in 1989 are won by SWAPO, leading to independence in 1990 under Owambo president Sam Nujoma.

1989   F. W. De Klerk becomes President of South Africa and announces that he will abolish racial discrimination.

Rhodesian prime minister Ian Smith signs the Unilateral Declaration of Independence in 1965. This attempt to maintain white-minority rule was in response to British plans to introduce voting rights for Africans.

1990 Nelson Mandela is released after 27 years in prison.

1992 Formal peace agreement established in Mozambique.

1993 For their work in ending apartheid, Mandela and de Klerk are jointly awarded the Nobel Peace Prize.

1994 South Africa holds its first all-race elections, which are won overwhelmingly by Nelson Mandela and the ANC. As president, Mandela establishes the Truth and Reconciliation Commission (TRC) which investigates human rights violations under apartheid. The new government also begins housing, education, and economic development reforms to improve the living standards of the country's black population.

1998 Street protests at fraudulent election in Lesotho; neighbors Botswana, South Africa, and Zimbabwe are called upon to restore order. Plan announced in Zimbabwe by Robert Mugabe for the redistribution of farmland, involving the seizure of more than 800 white-owned farms.

1999 In Zimbabwe the Movement for Democratic Change (MDC) under leader Morgan Tsvangirai is launched to protest the massive inflation and social problems brought about by President Robert Mugabe's policies. Thabo Mbeki is elected president of South Africa.

2000 Zimbabwean Supreme Court rules that government land reform plans and seizure of white-owned farms are illegal.

Three South African presidents, spanning the period from white rule to the start of the 21st century. From right to left: F. W. De Klerk, the Afrikaner Nationalist leader who ended the apartheid system; Nelson Mandela of the ANC, the first president elected by all South Africans; and Thabo Mbeki, Mandela's successor.

2001 International pressure forces multinational drug companies to end their legal battle to stop South Africa importing cheaper "nonbrand" drugs to combat the spread of AIDS.

2002 In Zimbabwe, MDC leader Morgan Tsvangirai is arrested for treason; he is acquitted on all charges two years later. Persecution by Mugabe supporters continues. In presidential elections, Mugabe beats Tsvangirai in a poll widely condemned as fraudulent.

2003 U.S. president George Bush imposes economic sanctions on Zimbabwe for human rights abuses.

2004 Widespread drought across southern Africa affects South Africa, Zimbabwe, Lesotho, and Malawi. Food shortages bring threat of famine. In Zimbabwe, Robert Mugabe stops food aid from reaching his opponents. South Africa's third free elections bring an increase in the ANC's share of the vote (70 percent). 5 million South Africans—some 11 percent of the population—are reported to be infected with AIDS.

2005 ZANU-PF again wins a majority in Zimbabwe, but the vote is marred by intimidation and violence.

MAJOR WORKS AND THEIR AUTHORS

Title	Date	Author	Language
Klokgrassies (Bell Grasses)	1914	D. F. Malherbe	Afrikaans
Chaka (King Shaka)	1925	Thomas Mafolo	Sesotho
Insila kaShaka (King Shaka's Bodyservant)	1930	John Dube	Zulu
Diphosho-phosho (The Comedy of Errors)	1930	Solomon Plaatje	Setswana
Noma nini (Forever and Ever)	1935	Benedict Vilakazi	Zulu
Alleenspraak (Soliloquy)	1935	N. P. van Wyk Louw	Afrikaans
U-Dingane kaSenzangakhona (King Dingaan, Son of Senzangakhona)	1936	R. R. R Dhlomo	Zulu
Ingqumbo Yeminyanya (The Wrath of the Ancestors)	1940	A. C. Jordan	Xhosa
Inkinsela yaseMgungundlovu (The Wealthy Man from Pietermaritzburg)	1961	Sibusiso Nyembezi	Zulu
Rook en oker (Smoke and Ocher)	1963	Ingrid Jonker	Afrikaans
Kennis van die Aand (Looking on Darkness)	1973	André P. Brink	Afrikaans
Magagana (Battle Ax)	1974	D. M. Modise	Setswana
Ho tsamaea ke ho bona (To Travel Is To See)	1983	A. S. Mopeli-Paulus	Sesotho
Isahluko Sokugqibela (The Last Chapter)	2000	Zibele Sisusa	Xhosa

THE HISTORY OF LITERATURE IN SOUTHERN AFRICAN LANGUAGES BEGINS WITH THE ORAL LITERATURES OF INDIGENOUS PEOPLES. STORYTELLING IN WRITTEN FORMS OF AFRICAN LANGUAGES ONLY DEVELOPED AFTER EUROPEAN CONTACT. THIS PROCESS WAS DRIVEN BY EFFORTS TO SPREAD CHRISTIANITY.

EARLY HISTORY

There are few written records of precolonial literature in southern Africa, since it was all transmitted orally (see ORAL LITERATURE). In medieval times, some parts of southern Africa had experienced limited contact with writing in the form of the script used by Arab settlers and traders from the east coast. However, it was only after the arrival of European colonists from the mid-17th century onward that written forms of the various southern African languages were developed. In each case, pioneering linguists transposed the sounds of the African languages into the Roman alphabet, so enabling the African languages to be written down for the first time. The European settlers also brought printing presses with them, which allowed them to produce and distribute literature in southern African languages on a wide scale.

THE ROLE OF MISSIONARY SOCIETIES

Throughout southern Africa, the earliest literary works in African languages were almost always published by missionary societies. From the 19th century onward,

Missionary societies played a major role in the development of written forms of African languages. Here, a missionary reads aloud to Africans from the Bible.

more and more missionary societies arrived in the region. In order to spread their beliefs more widely, they first set up printing presses and then commissioned and published translations of various religious works. Consequently, many of the first publications in African languages were religious in nature. For example, Xhosa written literature began with the foundation of the Lovedale Press, established by the Glasgow Mission Society of the Church of Scotland in 1823, which published translations of the Ten Commandments and the Lord's Prayer. The first literary work in Xhosa was a translation of John Bunyan's *Pilgrim's Progress* by the Xhosa scholar Tiyo Soga (1829–71), which was published in 1870.

NATIONALISM AND DECOLONIZATION

Alongside these religious texts, African language publications also included works of a nationalist character, such as the historical novels of R. R. R. Dhlomo (1906–71), which were based on the lives of 19th-century Zulu rulers. African-language literature provided an important forum for airing anticolonial views. However, because the parties and leaders that first emerged in southern African countries after the end of colonialism had an anti-racist ideology, they did not encourage the development of literature that celebrated linguistic and ethnic differences. From a different perspective, black writers in South Africa believed that they could most effectively oppose the apartheid government by using English as the medium to put across their message. To write in a variety of African languages, each of them understood by only part of the populace, seemed to them to be playing along with the "divide and rule" policy of the Bantu Education Act.

Indeed, the small potential readership for literary works in these languages has continued to be a major stumbling-block for the development of African-language literature; far wider markets are open to works in European languages. To try and counteract this trend, there is at present a drive in countries such as South Africa and Botswana to develop the African-language literatures of the region. New literary talents have emerged, such as the Xhosa author Zibele Sisusa (b.1964), whose first novel, a work for young adult readers, won a literary award in 2000.

AFRIKAANS LITERATURE

Although not an African language in the strictest sense, the fact that Afrikaans has undergone centuries of development in southern Africa means that it can be regarded as such. Literary endeavors in Afrikaans only began relatively recently, in the first decades of the 20th century.

In the 1960s a group of prominent Afrikaans authors known as the *Sestigers* (People of the Sixties) championed the cause of art for art's sake, and were widely criticized for avoiding the burning political issues generated by apartheid. But from the 1970s onward, works by Afrikaans authors such as André P. Brink (b.1935) and Breyten Breytenbach (b.1939) began to challenge the apartheid regime. Afrikaans continues to be a vibrant literary language today.

The author Breyten Breytenbach, an outspoken critic of the South African apartheid regime, was jailed for seven years for his views. He has written poetry, novels, and essays in both Afrikaans and English.

SEE ALSO: *Afrikaners; English-language literature; Oral literature; Sotho; Zulu.*

THE MORIJA PRESS

Founded in Lesotho in 1833 by the Paris Evangelical Missionary Society, the Morija Press played a pioneering role in the publication of Sesotho (Southern Sotho) books and remains one of the largest Sesotho-language publishers. A Sesotho-language newspaper, *Leselinyana la Lesotho* (The Light of Lesotho), founded by the mission in 1863, has continued to appear ever since, though it is now under new ownership. As well as producing religious texts, the Morija Press was also responsible for publishing the first Sesotho novel, *Chaka*, by Thomas Mofolo, in 1925.

AFRIKANERS

FACT FILE

Population	2,500,000 in South Africa, 100,000 in Namibia, 6,000 in Botswana, and smaller numbers elsewhere
Religion	Christianity (Dutch Reformed Church)
Language	Afrikaans, a creole language, is essentially a simplified form of Dutch, and was originally called Cape Dutch. Its grammar and vocabulary have been enriched by influences from Malay and various African languages.

TIMELINE

1652	Jan van Riebeeck establishes station at the Cape for Dutch East India Company.
1795–1806	British invade and take control of the Cape Colony, where 15,000 Afrikaners are living.
1835–54	Voortrekkers journey inland from the Cape.
1843	British annex Boer state of Natalia (Natal).
1881	British annex Transvaal; British defeat in the First Anglo-Boer War ensures Transvaal's independence.
1899–1902	Second Anglo-Boer War; 450,000 British troops finally defeat 80,000 Boers.
1910	Union of South Africa established.
1925	Afrikaans replaces Dutch as an official language.
1948	The National Party wins power in South Africa.
1961	South Africa becomes a republic.
1976	A major black uprising begins in the township of Soweto, Johannesburg.
1989–90	Nationalist president F. W. de Klerk elected; he announces an end to apartheid and unbans the black opposition party, the African National Congress (ANC).
1994	ANC under Nelson Mandela (imprisoned for 27 years under apartheid) wins power in South Africa.

AFRIKANERS—A DUTCH WORD MEANING "AFRICANS"— ARE A WHITE TRIBE THAT CAME TOGETHER IN SOUTH AFRICA FROM A MIX OF DUTCH, GERMAN, AND FRENCH PROTESTANT (HUGUENOT) SETTLERS AS WELL AS LOCAL PEOPLES. AFRIKANER NATIONALISM INTRODUCED THE APARTHEID SYSTEM IN SOUTH AFRICA.

HISTORY

The Afrikaner nationalist movement was born out of a history of oppositions: against the Dutch East India Company, first against the indigenous Khoikhoi peoples, then against Bantu-speaking peoples of the interior and finally, and perhaps most importantly, against the British Empire. The Second Anglo-Boer War of 1899–1902 was a key event in the rise of Afrikaner nationalism. To counter effective Boer guerrilla tactics, the British cleared Boer farms and imprisoned Afrikaner families in concentration camps, where 26,000 people, mainly women and children, died of disease. When Afrikaner nationalists (many of whom had enthusiastically supported Nazi Germany in World War II) came to power in South Africa in 1948, they brought in the system of racial segregation known as apartheid. People were classified by the color of their skin and forced to live in separate areas according to race, mixed marriages were banned, and educational and other life opportunities were systematically denied to the majority black population.

Recently, some Afrikaners have suggested that apartheid's classification of Afrikaans speakers with darker skins as "Coloured" was an artificial division, and have instead promoted an Afrikanerdom that includes these people as well.

SOCIETY AND DAILY LIFE

The term *Boer* means "farmer," reflecting the strong rural base of the Afrikaans-speaking population. Afrikaners began farming in the Cape when the Dutch East India Company granted land to immigrants to grow crops and raise stock to sell to the Company. A way of life developed in which large tracts of land were farmed by Afrikaner families, with the help of a large workforce of African people. As the population grew, so did the hunger for land and an independent farming life on the frontier.

Pioneer farmers known as Trekboers developed a migratory way of life—herding livestock and living by hunting—that differed little from (and also drew extensively upon) that of their Khoikhoi servants. After the Anglo-Boer War ended in 1902, many poor Boers were forced to quit the land for the towns, where they had to compete for work with African people and speak in English. This fed Afrikaner nationalism, which tried to solve the so-called "poor-white problem." Today, since the legal advantages that white people had

An Afrikaner family in traditional dress celebrates the heritage of the Voortrekkers. On the Great Trek of 1835–36, these pioneers traveled inland, fleeing British rule. After fighting the Zulus and Ndebele, they founded the Orange Free State, Transvaal, and Natalia (KwaZulu-Natal) in eastern South Africa.

The massive granite Voortrekker monument near Pretoria is a shrine of Afrikaner nationalism. Sited high on a hill, it can be seen for many miles in all directions. Inside, a marble frieze shows scenes from the Great Trek.

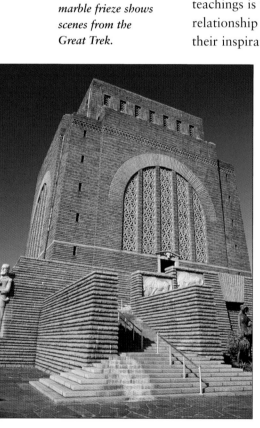

during apartheid have been removed, some Afrikaners are once again facing unemployment and poverty in the cities of South Africa.

CULTURE AND RELIGION

Most Afrikaners are members of the Christian Dutch Reformed Church, which was founded in 1618 and is based on the doctrines of John Calvin. Central to its teachings is the idea that God has a special relationship with certain peoples. Taking their inspiration from the Bible, many Afrikaners likened their own position in southern Africa to that of the Israelites in the Old Testament; they saw themselves as chosen by God to found their own state and bring Christian order and light to "darkness."

On December 16, 1838, before the Battle of Blood River against the Zulus, the Voortrekker leaders made a covenant with God, as Abraham had done in the Old Testament, that they would consecrate a church and celebrate the day with thanksgiving if he saved them. The Afrikaners understood their victory to be a sign of

THE VOORTREKKER MONUMENT

The construction of this huge monument took place between 1938 and 1949, at the height of Afrikaner nationalism. It was built to celebrate the Voortrekkers who had embarked on the Great Trek, leaving the Cape Colony in their thousands between 1835 and 1854 to avoid the ban on slave ownership that the British authorities at the Cape had imposed. On December 16 each year at noon, commemorating the victorious Battle of Blood River in 1838, a ray of light shines down on a cenotaph in the main hall, illuminating carved words from the country's former National Anthem "Die Stem": *Ons vir Jou, Suid-Afrika* (We for thee, South Africa).

God's approval; they claimed the land in the interior had been granted to them by God.

The Afrikaner Nationalist movement was later to elaborate on this mythology and to create a series of ceremonies and monuments that celebrated the legendary history of the Volk (*people*) as a way of uniting a number of previously distinct Afrikaans-speaking communities. For example, the Taal Monument at Paarl, near Cape Town, was built to celebrate the Afrikaans language. Yet the most solemn ceremony was the annual observance of the Day of the Covenant on December 16, which was made a national

The ox-wagon, as used by the Voortrekkers, is an iconic emblem of Afrikanerdom. Sixty-four wagons were drawn up in a circular laager (camp) before the Battle of Blood River. Here, members of the white supremacist Afrikaner Weerstands-beweging (AWB; "Afrikaner Resistance Movement") attend a rally at a laager monument. It was feared that the AWB, who represent a small minority of Afrikaners, would disrupt South Africa's first free elections in 1994, but the threat came to nothing.

holiday across South Africa in 1910. This was renamed the Day of Reconciliation after 1994, when the apartheid period ended.

Yet it would be wrong to identify all Afrikaners with conservative politics and traditional Dutch Reformed Church values. Many leading Afrikaans-speaking writers such as André P. Brink (b.1935), Breyten Breytenbach (b.1939), and J. M. Coetzee (b.1940), were outspoken critics of the inhumane policy of apartheid.

SEE ALSO: *English-speaking Southern Africans; "Cape Coloured" people/Cape Malays; Christianity; Khoikhoi; Xhosa; Zulu.*

THE BROEDERBOND

A key aspect of Afrikaner nationalism was the secret society known as the Afrikaner Broederbond (League of Afrikaner Brothers). This all-white, all-male organization, established in 1919, was dedicated to promoting the interests of Afrikaners over the English-speaking community and ensuring that Afrikaners took and held on to power in South Africa. It offered vital support in the creation of the ultra-conservative Herenigde Nasionale Party (HNP: Purified National Party) under the leadership of D. F. Malan in 1933. During the National Party's rule, between 1948 and 1994, every prime minister and state president belonged to the Broederbond. In 1993, the Broederbond ended its secrecy and, now renamed the Afrikanerbond, allowed women and even other races as members.

BUILDING TECHNIQUES

Zulu Kraal: reed and wicker beehive houses built around a central cattle enclosure.

Xhosa Adobe houses with thatched roofs. Settlements grouped around a central point, but with no formal structure.

Ndebele Historically adobe houses with ocher geometric designs. Brick houses and acrylic paints in recent times.

Venda Similar to Xhosa houses, but with addition of overhanging thatched roof for shade. Villages often built on elevated promontories for defensive purposes.

Nama (Khoikhoi descendants) Simple wicker frameworks with removable hides or reed mats. Well suited to seminomadic life.

Dutch colonists Cape Dutch farmstead: single-story, gabled, and plastered houses; often built in an H shape.

Traditional adobe-walled and thatch-roofed houses of the Sotho people, re-created at the Basotho Cultural Village in Qwa-Qwa National Park, South Africa. Later Sotho architecture incorporates colorful house-painting techniques similar to those of the Ndebele.

A GREAT VARIETY OF BUILDING STYLES DEVELOPED IN SOUTHERN AFRICA. THEIR FORM AND ARRANGEMENT WERE DICTATED BY THE MATERIALS THAT WERE AVAILABLE AND THE WAY IN WHICH DIFFERENT SOCIETIES WERE ORGANIZED. UNDER THE IMPACT OF MODERNIZATION, MANY OF THE TRADITIONAL ARCHITECTURAL STYLES ARE BEING REPLACED BY MORE STANDARDIZED WAYS OF BUILDING.

ARCHITECTURE AND POWER

The most famous example of large-scale indigenous architecture in southern Africa is Great Zimbabwe, in the southeast of the modern state of Zimbabwe (see SHONA). Archaeologists and historians believe that

the impressive stone structures here are the remains of a once wealthy and powerful city built by the ancestors of the modern Shona. Great Zimbabwe flourished as a center of trade with the merchants of the East African coast between the 13th and 15th centuries. The outer walls of the site's Great Enclosure were built using no mortar or cement and have survived up to the present day, standing 34 feet (10 m) at their highest. These sturdy structures were decorated with inlaid "herring-bone" designs and were topped by grand soapstone carvings, only some of which now remain. Inside the Great Enclosure a large conical tower is also still standing. This building is thought to represent the king's granary, but may well have been more than a simple grain store, acting as a potent symbol of the king's power by showing that he had access to food even in times of severe famine.

Among the Zulu of South Africa, kingly or chiefly power also played a significant role in the development of dwellings. Mgungundlovu, the royal capital of the Zulu ruler Dingaan (d.1843), consisted of some 1,700 beehive-shaped huts built in concentric rings around a central cattle enclosure. This classic Zulu layout is widely known by its Afrikaans name kraal (corral). In the past Zulu houses were made of reeds tied and woven onto a wicker framework. Their floors were a mixture of cow dung and blood that, once dry, could be polished and brought to a shine. In the present-day province of KwaZulu-Natal, however, brick and cement houses are most common.

EVOLVING STYLES

The Ndebele have also abandoned their traditional mud-and-timber architecture, but they continue to incorporate decorative forms into their modern brick houses. Their homes, whose external walls are covered with colorful geometric designs, recall older decorative traditions, such as the engraving

SHANTYTOWNS

Shantytowns are by no means unique to southern Africa—Brazil has its favelas, and the Philippines its barrios. However, in South Africa in the late 20th century, shantytowns such as those at Cape Flats became a powerful symbol of the deliberate injustice of the apartheid system (notably the 1950 Group Areas Act, which forced black people to quit "white" neighborhoods). Poverty, crime, and a severe lack of basic amenities like drainage and running water characterize these squatter settlements. The building materials used for the makeshift houses there include corrugated iron and other scrap metals, plastic bags, chipboard, wood, wire, tire rubber, and discarded packing crates. Yet squalor and deprivation is not the whole story; many South African shantytowns have become centers of great pride for their inhabitants. Several craft skills (see CONTEMPORARY ART) are needed to put up a shanty house, and accordingly shantytowns have grown into centers of a thriving craft-work industry. Despite the very poor standard of living, the vitality and strong sense of community in shantytowns continue to inspire local artists, musicians, and poets.

and stippling of walls with chevrons, zig-zags, and diamond shapes. These patterns are common to Ndebele crafts; once acrylic paints became available in the 1960s, wall painters began to use bright colors instead of earth tones to mimic Ndebele beadwork.

In many societies the architecture of a person's home reflects changes in her or his social standing. Among the Zafimaniry of Madagascar, house-building is a lifelong process that begins with marriage. The houses of newlyweds have walls made of flimsy reed mats, but married couples with several children are entitled to replace these, over time, with wooden panels carved with intricate designs that are meant to bring good fortune. Accordingly, people who have been married longest and have had the greatest number of children have the strongest and most ornate houses.

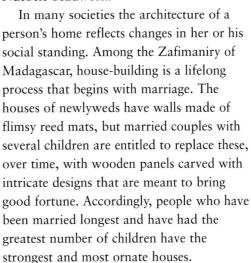

A South African shantytown—at Secunda in Mpumalanga province—with its makeshift homes. One of the biggest challenges facing postapartheid governments in South Africa is to improve housing conditions. In 2005, Secunda and many other shantytowns across the country were the scene of major protests against poor sanitation and water supply.

SEE ALSO: Contemporary art; Ndebele and Matabele; Sotho; Zulu.

"CAPE COLOURED" PEOPLE/CAPE MALAYS

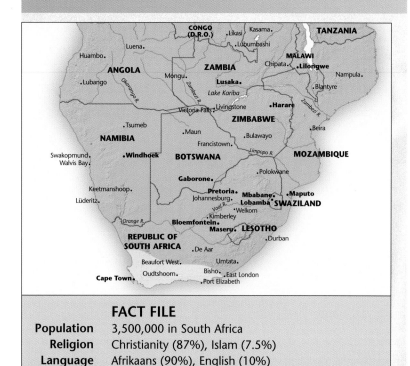

FACT FILE

Population	3,500,000 in South Africa
Religion	Christianity (87%), Islam (7.5%)
Language	Afrikaans (90%), English (10%)

TIMELINE

1652	Dutch sailor Jan van Riebeeck founds a fort at Table Bay on behalf of the Dutch East India Company.
1658	The first large shipment of slaves arrives at the Cape from the Dutch East Indies (Indonesia and Malaysia).
1795–1806	Britain takes control of the Cape from the Dutch.
1828	"Freemen of color" granted equal rights in the Cape.
1838	Full emancipation of slaves in the British Empire.
1853	Right to vote extended to all citizens, dependent on economic circumstances.
1910	Union of South Africa gives Coloured People in the Cape the vote, but by 1930 they are restricted to electing white representatives.
1948	Election of National Party sees all Coloured People eventually deprived of their right to vote.
1950	Group Areas Act creates separate areas for Cape Coloured people.
1966	District Six (in central Cape Town) declared a white area.
1983	Coloured People allowed to vote for a separate parliament.
1994	First free elections, won by the African National Congress (ANC), see the National Party retain control of the Western Cape.
2004	ANC takes control of the Western Cape Province.

SOUTH AFRICA'S CAPE REGION IS HOME TO THE CAPE COLOURED AND CAPE MALAY COMMUNITIES. CAPE COLOURED PEOPLE ARE OF MIXED AFRICAN, EUROPEAN, AND ASIAN DESCENT. CAPE MALAYS TRACE THEIR ORIGINS TO SOUTHEAST ASIA. THE TWO GROUPS PRACTICE DIFFERENT RELIGIONS.

HISTORY

The term *Coloured* was used during the apartheid period in South Africa to classify people of unclear or mixed descent. It was a catch-all term embracing a number of different sections of the Afrikaans- and English-speaking communities that were not recognized as racially white.

The history of South Africa's population with a mixed-race heritage is linked to the history of the Cape under Dutch and later British rule, where native Khoikhoi and San peoples mingled with slaves and convicts from Southeast Asia, Madagascar, and East Africa. Various groups within the community emphasize different aspects of their ancestry.

One of the most distinct groups are the Cape Malays. The first political prisoners from the Dutch East Indies were brought to Cape Town from 1658, where a population of around 150,000 has survived, united by their Muslim faith.

SOCIETY AND DAILY LIFE

Historical ways of life for members of the Cape Coloured community included working as fishers, in domestic service, or as farm laborers. Many Cape Coloured People in the Western and Northern Cape Provinces still perform these roles, but others lead professional lives as doctors or lawyers, for example, and enjoy an urban lifestyle little different than that of their neighbors.

Dancers in their bright satin uniforms take part in the Cape Town Minstrel Carnival, the yearly celebration of Cape Coloured identity. The carnival has its roots in popular visits by minstrel troupes from the United States to the area in the early 1800s.

The imposition of the Group Areas Act in the 1950s and 1960s, which was designed to segregate the races under the policy of apartheid, saw the resettlement of many Coloured people into purpose-built townships. This created high unemployment and other social problems, still present today.

CULTURE AND RELIGION

Most Cape Coloured People are Christians, and many belong to the Dutch Reformed Church. Cape Malays are Muslim; the first mosque was established in Cape Town in the 1790s.

Culturally and politically, Cape Coloured People have much in common with Afrikaners. In South Africa's first multiethnic elections in 1994, and in 1999, the Western Cape Province returned National Party representatives, despite a national ANC landslide. Cape Coloured voters saw the ANC as favoring the black majority.

A major annual event for Cape Town's community is the Minstrel Carnival. Taking place in early January, it recalls the one day per year that slaves were granted for their own recreation. Today, the festival commemorates the freeing of the slaves in the Cape region. The carnival is organized by *klopse*—clubs that compete by performing politically satirical songs.

DISTRICT SIX

District Six was named as a district of Cape Town in 1867. Close to the city center and port and a central location for the Cape Coloured population, it was a lively area inhabited by freed slaves, merchants, artisans, laborers, and immigrants and their descendants. As such, it flew in the face of apartheid ideology as living proof of people's capacity to coexist in harmony. In 1966, District Six was designated a "white" area under the Group Areas Act, and 60,000 people were forcibly removed so that the quarter could be bulldozed. In 1999 the District Six Museum opened, commemorating the area's former inhabitants.

SEE ALSO: Afrikaners; English-speaking Southern Africans; Festival and ceremony; Khoikhoi; Xhosa.

TIMELINE

1505   First Christian church erected in southern Africa by the Portuguese, in Mozambique.

1652   Dutch introduce Christianity to South Africa on founding Cape Town.

1799   Under British rule multiple missionary societies begin work in the Cape Colony and beyond.

1816   Establishment of mission stations at Kuruman (among the Tswana) and in 1833 at Morija (among the Sotho).

1879   Anglican bishop John W. Colenso of Natal protests the British invasion of Zululand.

1881   Dutch Reformed Church establishes a separate "daughter church" for nonwhite congregations.

1910   Zionist Christian Church established.

1982   Apartheid condemned as a heresy by the World Council of Reformed Churches.

1984   Archbishop Desmond Tutu of Cape Town awarded the Nobel Peace Prize.

1985   The inter-faith Kairos document calls upon South Africans to support civil disobedience in the struggle against apartheid.

1994   New South African constitution guarantees freedom of religion.

2000s   Church leaders speak out against abuses in Zimbabwe.

INTRODUCED INTO SOUTHERN AFRICA BY PORTUGUESE EXPLORERS AT THE END OF THE 15TH CENTURY, CHRISTIANITY IS NOW THE MOST WIDELY PRACTICED RELIGION ACROSS THE REGION. IT HAS ADAPTED AND GROWN MORE VIBRANT BY INCORPORATING TRADITIONAL BELIEFS, AND HAS OFTEN BEEN A FORCE FOR SOCIAL CHANGE.

EARLY HISTORY

Christianity had a slow start in southern Africa. The Portuguese in Mozambique tried but largely failed to convert the rulers of the Mutapa kingdom of northern Zimbabwe to Roman Catholicism. The Dutch brought their own Calvinist Dutch Reformed Church to Cape Town in 1652 but banned missionary activity. Neither group of early settlers attempted mass conversion of Africans.

Zion Christian Church members gather for an open-air service in Pietermaritzburg. The ZCC is Africa's fastest-growing church.

THE ZION CHRISTIAN CHURCH (ZCC)

A characteristic feature of the growth of Christianity in southern Africa is the way in which indigenous African churches have developed independently of the major European denominations. Often, the members of these churches build African religious practices into their worship. The largest of these independent African churches is the Zion Christian Church, which was founded by a farm laborer, Engenas Lekganyane in 1910. Its members are now thought to number as many as 6 million, many of whom gather every Easter at the church's headquarters at Zion City in South Africa's Limpopo Province. The ZCC stresses the healing power of religious faith but respects African beliefs about the important role played by ancestors in daily life. It also maintains a strict moral code and encourages nonviolence.

MISSIONARY ACTIVITY

This situation changed radically in the 19th century, as Christianity ceased being a small-scale and exclusively white religion. Missionary societies were admitted when the British took over the Cape and promptly sought converts in the South African interior. They also actively promoted European values and material culture, including new styles of dress and farming practices. For this reason, African rulers often welcomed missionaries, notably in Madagascar and Lesotho. Yet many rulers did not immediately convert themselves, for fear of alienating their subjects, who mostly clung to preexisting beliefs. Some missionaries, such as David Livingstone, played a vital role in European exploration of Africa and in campaigns to abolish the slave trade. Others, like John Philip, fought for more equal treatment of black and mixed-race peoples. The growth of literacy in African languages was an important development, with mission presses at Kuruman (South Africa) and Morija (Lesotho) printing translations of the Bible and other Church literature.

THE CHURCH AND SOCIETY

As South Africa in particular became ever more racially divided, many church members condemned inequality, causing a rift among Christian denominations. The Dutch Reformed Church, for example, established separate congregations and (from 1881) segregated "daughter churches" for nonwhite members. Later, its leaders gave theological support to apartheid. But other Christian churches vehemently attacked the system as fundamentally un-Christian. The South African Council of Churches and leaders such as Archbishop Desmond Tutu were very active in the antiapartheid movement.

Christian churches and their leaders still play a key role in civil society in southern Africa today. In some countries, such as Lesotho, they provide essential education

and health services, especially in remote rural areas. They also champion human rights (e.g., in Zimbabwe), and are at the forefront of the fight against AIDS. Desmond Tutu is an outspoken critic of the South African government's stance on these issues.

NUMBERS

It is hard to know exactly how many Christians there are in the various countries of southern Africa. Certainly, the vast majority of South Africans are Christians. Most are Protestant, with the Dutch Reformed Church the largest single denomination (c. 4 million). Other large Protestant denominations are the Anglicans, Methodists, Lutherans, and Presbyterians. Over 3 million South Africans are Roman Catholics, a faith that also predominates in Lesotho and (despite years of persecution under Marxism) in Mozambique.

The church choir of Tiger Kloof school near Vryburg in North-West Province, South Africa. Established by the London Missionary Society in 1904, Tiger Kloof gave black pupils a full academic and vocational education for over 50 years. It was forced to close under apartheid, but resumed its work in 1995.

See also: Afrikaners; English-speaking Southern Africans; Sotho.

ARTISTS IN SOUTH AFRICA

Artist	Dates	Style/medium
Anton Anreith	1754–1821	Sculptor
Anton van Wouw	1862–1945	Realist sculptor
Jacob H. Pierneef	1886–1957	Landscape painter
Maggie Laubser	1886–1973	Painter (German Expressionist influence)
Irma Stern	1894–1966	Painter (German Expressionist influence)
Walter Battiss	1906–82	Painter
Alexis Preller	1911–75	Painter
Gerard Sekoto	1913–93	Painter
Cecil Skotnes	b.1926	Wood carver and engraver
Sydney Kumalo	1935–88	Sculptor
William Kentridge	b.1955	Painter, sketcher, moviemaker

THERE ARE TWO MAIN FORMS OF CONTEMPORARY ART IN SOUTHERN AFRICA. THE FIRST IS LOCALLY PRODUCED ART, WHILE THE SECOND IS A TRADITION BASED ON THE PRINCIPLES OF EUROPEAN FINE ART. THERE IS MUCH OVERLAP BETWEEN THESE CATEGORIES.

TRADITIONAL CRAFTS

The earliest southern African craft manufacture developed in the Iron Age among Bantu speakers and Khoikhoi groups. Craft traditions include basket weaving (for example, Zulu and Xhosa), beadwork (Zulu, Ndebele, and Khoikhoi), earthenware and ceramics (Bantu and Khoikhoi), decorative painting (Ndebele house painting), and wood and stone carving (Shona).

Among these peoples, craft objects were made both as practical items for daily use and for ritual use. From the early 20th century onward, such objects increasingly found their way into the cabinets of European collectors.

Tswana basketwork is a sophisticated art form. Basketmakers, who are exclusively women, use many different weaves to produce a huge variety of designs. Some are personal to the weaver, while other standard designs have evocative names like "Tears of the Giraffe" or "Forehead of the Zebra."

These African "oddities" had a huge impact on modern art in Europe, as painters and sculptors incorporated elements of what they saw as primitive art into their works.

More recently, craft items have found a new and very profitable outlet in the fast-growing tourist trade. Township craftwork is much in demand, and skilled craftspeople can earn a living by turning waste materials into offbeat art objects. Examples of such creations are elephants made from soda cans, chickens from supermarket plastic bags, and models of transistor radios, airplanes, and cars made from pieces of scrap wire and metal.

FINE ARTS

European fine art first appeared in southern Africa in the 18th century, when early travelers sketched the Cape landscape. For example, the German watercolorist Johannes Schumacher produced an early panoramic view of the Cape Town settlement in 1776–77. But this distinctly European genre only really gained a firm foothold later, through the work of such artists as the Afrikaner painter Jacob Hendrik Pierneef (1886–1957), who became well-known for his stylized trees and his expansive, dramatic skyscapes.

Irma Stern (1894–1966) was one of the first southern African artists to move beyond landscape painting, preferring to paint human figures. Her many intimate portraits include such works as *Pondo Women* (1929).

The Johannesburg artist Cecil Skotnes (b.1926) employed traditional carving techniques in his sculpture, using earth tones common in regional craft work. In 1961 Skotnes helped found the Amadlozi (Spirit of the Ancestors) group, the first South African artistic movement to admit black artists. The sculptor Sydney Kumalo (1935–88), another founder of the group, was known for the elongated forms and flowing lines in his work.

The northern Sotho artist Gerard Sekoto (1913–93) was known for his paintings of South African urban life. In the late 1930s, his pictures captured the vibrant life of the poor, multicultural Johannesburg township of Sophiatown. Frustrated by the lack of opportunities for black artists, he exiled himself to Paris in 1947, never to return.

Irma Stern was a South African artist who specialized in painting people. Her use of rich colors and bold brushstrokes—as in this painting, Bahuto Musicians *(1942)— creates a sense of great vitality.*

See also: Architecture; Khoikhoi; Ndebele and Matabele; Sculpture; Shona; Textiles; Tswana.

WILLIAM KENTRIDGE

The work of the Johannesburg artist William Kentridge is internationally acclaimed. After completing theater studies in Paris in 1981, Kentridge turned his hand to making movies. He was deeply affected by the injustices and atrocities of apartheid, such as the Sharpeville massacre of 1960, when police killed 69 unarmed black protestors outside a police station. His work became increasingly critical of the white-minority regime in his native country. His individual voice of protest and resistance was an inspiration for an emerging generation of artists and moviemakers. Their work aims to expose and challenge South Africa's painful history, and tries to reconcile the contradictions and inhumanity of its past with hope for the future. The Tate Modern gallery in London has a permanent exhibit of his work.

DANCE AND SONG

SONG AND DANCE STYLES

Song and Dance	Group or Tradition
Gumboot	Miners' work dance.
Indlamu	Zulu war dance and Swazi dance of feminine virtue.
Isicathamiya	South African acapella-type singing—popularized by Ladysmith Black Mambazo.
Jit	Zimbabwean vocal and percussion music—popularized by the Bhundu Boys in the 1980s.
Pantsula	South African township dance.
Tin Can Dance	Dance of complex rhythms created using ordinary tin cans.
Township Jive	Originated in Sophiatown, South Africa. Semi-acrobatic dance to typical 1950s South African Jazz/Rock 'n' Roll.

Gumboot dancers in South Africa. Because the mine workers who created this dance sang in Xhosa, Zulu, or Sotho, their white employers—who promoted dance troupes as a publicity stunt—did not understand the performers' subversive message.

S ONG AND DANCE ARE IMPORTANT MODES OF COMMUNICATION AMONG THE PEOPLES OF SOUTHERN AFRICA. DANCES INCORPORATE GESTURES, COSTUMES, MASKS, PROPS, BODY PAINTING, AND MANY OTHER STRIKING VISUAL ELEMENTS.

The expressive dynamism of South African dance forms is added to by the themes and symbols of the songs that usually accompany the dances. Together, dance and song create a dramatic occasion that reinforces cultural values, satisfies ritual and ceremonial demands, and sometimes even manages to touch on otherwise taboo subjects through the use of farce, mockery, and ridicule.

The various southern African Bantu-speaking peoples perform a number of dances that have strong similarities to one another. For example, the war dance known as *indlamu* among the Zulu is very similar to the *sibhaca* of the Swazi and a

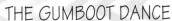

THE GUMBOOT DANCE

The energetic gumboot dance, or *isicathulo*, has gained worldwide recognition as a uniquely South African performance art. It originated in that county's gold mines as a response to the hardship and racial oppression that black workers regularly faced. In this difficult and dangerous environment, talking was impossible when noisy rock-drills were operating (and was also discouraged by the foremen), so miners worked out a way of communicating by tapping out different "codes" on the rubber gumboots they wore. After work, in their overcrowded hostels, the miners were banned from wearing traditional clothing, and so learned to adapt the dances and rhythms of the cultures they came from to their new surroundings, using their boots and bodies as instruments. The songs they wrote to accompany their complex stamping and slapping routines spoke of love, family, and friends, but also criticized low wages, harsh treatment, and poor working conditions.

war dance performed by the Shangaan (Tsonga). The Zulu *indlamu* dance, accompanied by drumming and whistling, is performed by men dressed in full battle regalia of animal skins, head rings, ceremonial belts and ankle rattles, and armed with spears and animal-hide shields. The dance is a celebration of Zulu military prowess on the battlefield, which began with their ruler Shaka's unification of the clans in 1816–20. It is a powerful expression of that people's sense of pride and independence.

Confusingly, the dance referred to as *indlamu* among the Swazi is quite different. It is a traditional dance that celebrates Swazi feminine beauty and virtue, and is performed by unmarried girls dressed only in beaded aprons and jewelry. The meanings of the songs sung to accompany it vary according to the occasion, but in all cases they help heighten the mood and impact of the dance.

The trance dance of the San people of the Kalahari is performed mostly by men, but also by women and very occasionally by both. Objects used in the dance include animal-hair fly whisks and ankle rattles. Most often, women clap and chant as men dance in a circle around an open fire. The repetitive rhythms of the dance and chants send the participants into a state of deep trance, in which they become possessed by the supernatural force known as *n/um*. When this happens, the dancers fling their arms behind them in a bent posture, sweat heavily, and bleed from the nose. The supernatural power generated by the dance is used by shamans (healers who mediate between the spirit world and people) to heal the sick and to ensure the well-being of the whole group.

EUROPEAN INFLUENCES AND EVOLVING STYLES

From as early as the end of the 17th century, slaves of many different nationalities were brought to the Cape Colony by Dutch settlers. They introduced many diverse styles of dance, song, and music, and many hybrid forms emerged. Later, European and American styles also had a strong influence on the dance styles enjoyed by these growing communities. In the 1950s, Sophiatown, a Johannesburg township, became the birthplace of township jive, South Africa's answer to American rock 'n' roll dancing. Other modern dance forms include *pantsula*, a modern township dance combining local rhythms with mime and well-known Western dance routines—for example, Gene Kelly's famous umbrella dance in the 1952 Hollywood musical *Singin' in the Rain*.

SEE ALSO: *Festival and ceremony; Music and musical instruments; San; Swazi; Tsonga; Zulu.*

In 2001, Thandi Nyandeni and Todd Twala, two women from the Soweto township in South Africa, formed a local dance troupe to perform the show Umoja, *which became a huge international hit. The lively and spectacular show (meaning "unity" in Swahili) tells the story of South African music and dance from ancient times to the present day.*

MAJOR WORKS AND THEIR AUTHORS

Title	Date	Author	Country
Ephemerides	1828	Thomas Pringle	South Africa
The Story of an African Farm	1883	Olive Schreiner	South Africa
Mhudi	1930	Sol Plaatje	South Africa
Cry, the Beloved Country	1948	Alan Paton	South Africa
Boesman and Lena	1969	Athol Fugard	South Africa
Maru	1971	Bessie Head	Botswana
The Conservationist	1974	Nadine Gordimer	South Africa
No Baby Must Weep	1975	Mongane Wally Serote	South Africa
Amandla	1980	Miriam Tlali	South Africa
The Road	1982	Zakes Mda	South Africa
Nervous Conditions	1988	Tsitsi Dangarembga	Zimbabwe
Butterfly Burning	1998	Yvonne Vera	Zimbabwe
Disgrace	1999	J. M. Coetzee	South Africa
Thirteen Cents	2000	K. Sello Duiker	South Africa

Olive Schreiner's first novel The Story of an African Farm, *which she published under the male pseudonym Ralph Iron in 1883, was an immediate success. This work was South Africa's first novel, and provoked controversy for its feminist and anti-Christian standpoint. Schreiner also took an early stand against racism in South Africa.*

SOUTHERN AFRICA WAS THE FIRST REGION TO EXPERIENCE LARGE-SCALE EUROPEAN COLONIZATION AND MISSIONARY ACTIVITY. WRITERS SOON BEGAN TO ENGAGE WITH THE THEME OF THE RELATIONSHIP BETWEEN AFRICANS AND SETTLERS, AND REACHED THE WIDEST POSSIBLE AUDIENCE BY WRITING IN ENGLISH. THIS TOPIC WAS THROWN INTO SHARP FOCUS BY THE APARTHEID PERIOD IN SOUTH AFRICA; ENGLISH-LANGUAGE WRITERS OF ALL RACES PRODUCED POWERFUL CONDEMNATIONS OF THIS INHUMANE SYSTEM.

THE COLONIAL PERIOD

The history of southern African literature written in English begins with the first British occupation of the Cape Colony and the arrival of English-speaking settlers in 1820. Perhaps the most famous of the early authors was the Scottish poet Thomas Pringle (1789–1834), who spent six years at the Cape and celebrated the landscape and life of the colony in many of his poems. Pringle is sometimes called "the father of South African poetry."

One of the dominant themes of early colonial literature was the relationship between the settlers and the land, as typified by the 1883 novel *The Story of an African Farm* by Olive Schreiner (1855–1920), the first novel in English written by a southern African woman.

In addition to the writings of the European settlers, the black inhabitants of the region contributed to its English literature from a relatively early period. While many of the earliest literary works were religious—a product of the missionary

education that most black authors had received—their writings soon began to deal with the changes faced by African cultures and their relationships with the colonists. The first novel written in English by a black South African author was *Mhudi* (1930) by Sol Plaatje (1876–1932).

APARTHEID AND DECOLONIZATION

One of the most famous southern African novelists was Alan Paton (1903–88). His widely acclaimed novel *Cry, the Beloved Country* had as one of its themes the destructive impact of industrialization on African communities and their values. This novel marked a shift in focus among the region's authors, who began to write more and more about urban environments and experiences. Paton's novel also dealt with the terrible racial injustices in South Africa. *Cry, the Beloved Country* was published in 1948,

Alan Paton was an elder statesman of South African literature. His most famous work Cry, the Beloved Country *tells the story of a young man corrupted by city life and also of friendship between the races. The novel suggested that there was hope even in a society as deeply divided as apartheid South Africa.*

ZAKES MDA

Zakes Mda (b.1948) is one of the most distinguished South African authors of the postapartheid period. Mda's literary career began during apartheid with the publication of poems in South African magazines such as *Staffrider, The Voice,* and *Oduma.* His first collection of poems, *Bits of Debris,* was published in 1986. While living in the United States in 1984, Mda came to international attention as a playwright by winning the Christina Crawford Award for his drama *The Road.* In the years following the end of apartheid in 1990, Mda has begun to establish himself as a novelist, and his novels, which include *The Heart of Redness* (2000) and *The Madonna of Excelsior* (2002), have been widely praised, particularly for the way in which they blend magical and realistic elements.

YVONNE VERA

Yvonne Vera (1964–2005) was one of Zimbabwe's leading literary figures. She won the 1996 Commonwealth Writers' Prize for African Literature for her novel *Under the Tongue*. Her complex fiction describes the traumas and difficulties of Zimbabwe both before liberation and after independence. Vera also made it clear that she was writing from a woman's perspective—a major innovation in southern Africa, where English-language literature had long been dominated by male authors.

South Africa's first black periodical was Drum *magazine, which was famous for its investigative journalism and satire. Its reporters often came into conflict with the apartheid regime. In 1999, its former editor, Sylvester Stein, wrote his memoirs* Who Killed Mr Drum? *(later turned into a play), which tells the story of the pioneering magazine.*

the same year that the National Party introduced the apartheid system, which had a huge impact on southern African literature.

In the 1950s and 1960s, the increasingly vibrant township communities gave rise to a generation of black writers. Known as the "Drum generation" after a popular 1950s periodical, *Drum* magazine, these writers adopted an uncomplicated prose style to paint a vivid but truthful picture of black urban experience. Their works revealed a sleazy but exciting world of jazz, shebeens (illegal township bars), and gangsters. They also reflected their authors' frustrations. On the one hand, they were well-educated city dwellers whose lives were restricted by apartheid; on the other, they were alienated from their African roots, but did not want to be assimilated by white liberal culture.

Alongside these black writers, several white authors came to prominence in the 1960s and 1970s. Critical of apartheid, writers such as Nadine Gordimer (b.1923), André Brink (b.1935), Athol Fugard

(b.1932), and J. M. Coetzee (b.1940) wrote works reflecting the turmoil of the region that also had a wide international appeal.

Meanwhile, black authors emerging during the 1970s and 1980s were far more politically radical than their predecessors. Adopting the ideas of the Black Consciousness movement (led by Steve Biko, who was murdered by South African police in 1977), these writers were determined to reveal the devastating social and political harm caused by apartheid and to affirm their pride in black culture.

Writers in other southern African states shared the concerns of South African writers, rejecting white colonial values and heralding majority rule. Botswana's Bessie Head (1937–86) and Zimbabwe's Dambudzo Marechera (1952–87) were notable realist novelists who wrote about contemporary issues.

POSTCOLONIAL LITERATURE

In the postcolonial and postapartheid period many new works have emerged in southern Africa. Many still engage with the region's history of colonial oppression. This literary resurgence has been fueled by an expanding international market in literatures from former European colonies. Many recent works, by established authors and newcomers alike, make use of innovative and exciting forms of writing and try to create new ways of seeing southern Africa and its peoples.

J. M. COETZEE

Now regarded as South Africa's foremost writer, J. M. Coetzee published his first novel *Dusklands* in 1974 and won the Nobel Prize for Literature in 2003. Writing in a powerful but bleak narrative style, Coetzee is interested both in the power struggles that shape human societies and relationships, and also in topical literary debates. *Disgrace* (1999) tells of the scandalous downfall of an aging white professor, who flees Cape Town for the peace of his daughter's farm. In describing the tensions between the black and white rural inhabitants, Coetzee touches on difficult contemporary issues in South African society. It is a controversial novel that has generated much debate about the state of postapartheid South Africa.

SEE ALSO: African-language literature; Oral literature; Television and radio.

ENGLISH-SPEAKING SOUTHERN AFRICANS

English-speaking Southern Africans mainly inhabit major cities or their environs throughout the region.

FACT FILE

Population	1,715,000 in South Africa; 125,000 in Zimbabwe
Religion	Christianity
Languages	South African English can be easily understood by other English speakers, but incorporates a number of Afrikaans and African words.

TIMELINE

1806	British forces take permanent control of the Cape.
1820	5,000 British settlers arrive in South Africa, with the promise of fertile farmland.
1838	Final freeing of slaves throughout the British Empire.
1845	Natal annexed as a detached district of the Cape.
1867	Discovery of diamonds near Kimberley in Northern Cape Province leads to white settlement of the area and a major railroad building program.
1879–81	Defeat of British forces by the Zulu (at Isandhlwana) and Boers (Majuba Hill, in the first Anglo-Boer War).
1886	Discovery of gold in the Witwatersrand, Transvaal.
1890	British forces enter Mashonaland, later Zimbabwe.
1899–1902	Second Anglo-Boer War ends in British victory.
1910	Union of South Africa established.
1948	Afrikaner Nationalist government introduces apartheid.
1994	First nonracial elections in South Africa.
1995	The Truth and Reconciliation Commission (TRC) is set up under Archbishop Desmond Tutu to try and heal the scars left by apartheid.
2004	African National Congree (ANC) wins the country's third free general elections with 69 percent of the votes.

ENGLISH SETTLERS IN SOUTHERN AFRICA HAVE HISTORICALLY BEEN ASSOCIATED WITH THE REGION'S COMMERCIAL LIFE. IN SOUTH AFRICA, THEY SETTLED MAINLY IN CITIES, WHILE ELSEWHERE THEY DROVE THE FARMING ECONOMY. ENGLISH IS A WORLDWIDE LANGUAGE OF BUSINESS, AND AN INTERNATIONAL OUTLOOK HAS GREATLY BENEFITED THIS COMMUNITY.

HISTORY

British people first visited South Africa while traveling to Asia on trading voyages. Permanent British control of the Cape only began in 1806, with the first large influx of English settlers coming in 1820. The next major wave of English immigration to South Africa occurred in the late 19th century when diamonds and gold were discovered in the interior. The expansion of British control into the mineral-rich area of Mashonaland (now part of Zimbabwe) was stimulated by the commercial interests of the imperial entrepreneur Cecil Rhodes (1853–1902) and his British South Africa Company.

Many British soldiers who came to fight in the Anglo-Boer War of 1899–1902 also settled in South Africa. South Africa became independent from Britain in 1931, and the domination of government positions by Afrikaners during apartheid reinforced the commercial focus of much of the English-speaking South African population.

SOCIETY AND DAILY LIFE

Early English attempts at farming in South Africa were largely unsuccessful, and today the English-speaking population is now mainly an urban and commercial one. English speakers are concentrated in the

large cities of Cape Town, Durban, and Johannesburg and have long dominated the business sector.

Their relative wealth has given many English South Africans a high standard of living, and they are major employers of domestic servants. Although the nuclear family of parents and children is the normal residential pattern, live-in domestic servants may also form part of the household but generally live in separate quarters.

CULTURE AND RELIGION

While Afrikaner critics have pointed to the links that many English South Africans kept with their home country (supposedly making them less self-reliant), the country's long period of independence helped foster a strong sense of separate South African identity. This is most apparent at sporting events, where support for South Africa's rugby and cricket teams against England is very passionate.

As an internationally oriented community, the culture of English South Africans has tended to have a very cosmopolitan, international flavor in the arts, music, literature, and theater. However, some works

of art have engaged closely with local details of South African life. There is a strong tradition of English South African literature, which has won international acclaim.

Many of the early missionaries to Southern Africa were British and most English South Africans regard themselves as Christian, along with 80 percent of the rest of the population.

SEE ALSO: Afrikaners; English-language literature; Ndebele and Matabele; Shona; Xhosa; Zulu.

His face proudly painted with the flag of the multiracial "rainbow nation," which replaced the old South African flag in 1994, an English-speaking South African cheers for his team at the 2003 Rugby World Cup.

WHITE FARMERS IN ZIMBABWE

Alongside its mineral wealth, a mainstay of Zimbabwe's economy since colonization as Rhodesia from the late 19th century was its agriculture. The colonial government sold land that had been seized from the Shona and Matabele people to English-speaking white settlers, who set up large, successful farms. With independence and black majority rule from 1980 onward, one of the most pressing questions in Zimbabwe has been that of land redistribution to redress the injustices of colonialism. The ZANU-PF regime of Robert Mugabe encouraged the illegal and violent seizure of white-owned farms by so-called "war veterans," many of whom are far too young to have fought in the liberation struggle. The results have been a drastic fall in farm output (worsened by serious drought), famine in a once-plentiful country, and the destruction not just of white farmers' livelihoods but also those of thousands of black farm laborers.

MAJOR EVENTS IN SOUTHERN AFRICA

Swazi of Swaziland	The Incwala festival: "The festival of the First Fruits." The whole nation honors the king and receives blessings from the ancestors.	Dec/Jan: Confirmed by the tribal astronomers weeks before
Zulu of KwaZulu-Natal, South Africa	The Shembe Zulu festival: Started by the Baptist prophet Isaiah Shembe in around 1910. Thousands of people in traditional dress gather on the Inyesabe River. The Shembe slow dance is performed, accompanied by the blowing of the Horns of Jericho.	October
Tswana of Botswana, Zimbabwe, Namibia, and South Africa	The Bogwera and Bojale initiation ceremonies for adolescent boys and girls respectively. Following these ceremonies, the youths are accepted as responsible adults.	Middle to late adolescence
Ju/'hõansi San of the Kalahari Desert	The Eland Bull Dance is a ceremony of female initiation in which naked women are chased by two men (acting as eland bulls) around a hut in which lies the female initiate, who has experienced her first period.	At the start of puberty
Antakarana Kingdom of Madagascar	The Tsangan festival is the largest Antakarana festival. Its aim is to consecrate royal power, strengthening the links between the descendants of King Tsimiharo (1825–82). It includes feasting, animal sacrifice, and a pilgrimage to Mitsio Island and the Ankarana caves.	Dry season
Xhosa of the Eastern Cape, South Africa; Zulu	The lobola ceremony is carried out prior to the marriage of a couple. The groom is obliged to pay the bride's family in heads of cattle. The payment is followed by a feast in which one of the cattle is sacrificed in honor of the ancestors.	Before marriage

M ANY FESTIVALS AND CEREMONIES ARE HELD IN SOUTHERN AFRICA. SOME CELEBRATE SIGNIFICANT MOMENTS IN THE HISTORY OF A PEOPLE OR IN THE LIVES OF INDIVIDUALS, WHILE OTHERS MARK THE SEASONS. OTHER FESTIVALS COMMEMORATE PAST POLITICAL AND SOCIAL EVENTS, CELEBRATE THE PRESENT, OR LOOK FORWARD TO THE FUTURE.

RITES OF PASSAGE CEREMONIES

Many ceremonies concern major moments of change in an individual person's life, commonly referred to as rites of passage. These include birth, the move from childhood to adulthood, marriage, and death. Most southern African peoples celebrate the period when adolescents come of age with elaborate rites and ceremonies.

The male initiation into full adulthood, between the ages 15 and 18, often involves a circumcision ritual. Among the modern Xhosa of South Africa, the rite marking this life phase requires that the group of initiates leave their community and live in temporary shelters in the bush for three weeks. The initiates cover themselves with white clay and are allowed only a blanket to keep themselves warm. Once this ceremonial process is complete, the youths are regarded as men of worth who may occupy positions of social responsibility. The first president of a free South Africa, Nelson Mandela, who is a Xhosa, recalls this much-dreaded test of manhood in his autobiography *Long Walk to Freedom* (1994).

Young Xhosa men from South Africa's Eastern Cape province perform a dance celebrating their initiation into adulthood through the abakweta *circumcision ceremony.*

Often, important ceremonies involve not only initiates, but their families as well. The marriage ceremony of the seminomadic Himba people of Kunene, Namibia (see HERERO) requires the family of the groom to kidnap the bride before the official wedding rites are performed. Family members adorn her with an *ekori*—a headdress made of goatskin—instruct her in the responsibilities of being a wife, and smear her with butterfat. She is then accepted into the groom's family.

Death is frequently the occasion for the largest and most elaborate ceremony, in which whole communities may participate. During the funeral rites of the Madagascan Bara people, huge quantities of rum and beef are consumed in lively feasts that last for days.

CELEBRATING PAST EVENTS

Festivals and ceremonies sometimes commemorate key moments in a people's history, and accord the central characters of the event semi-heroic status. In South Africa, the apartheid government celebrated the landing of the first Dutch commander, Jan Van Riebeeck, at the Cape in 1652. Three hundred years after this event (which most South Africans had no reason to celebrate) a lavish reenactment of the landing was staged, with actors manning a replica of Van

THE CAPE TOWN MINSTREL CARNIVAL

One of South Africa's most high-profile festivals is the Cape Town Minstrel Carnival. It is a yearly celebration in which brightly dressed minstrels from Cape Town's Coloured community parade through the streets accompanied by big-band jazz groups and impressive floats. The participants belong to a number of *klopse*, or clubs, each with its own costume, banners, and mascots. The festival is an unofficial commemoration of Freedom Day, when slaves were emancipated at the Cape in 1834. The minstrel theme was introduced in 1848 when White American Dixie minstrels visited Cape Town and performed with their faces blackened by burnt cork. This tradition stuck among the former slave population, who composed songs and rhymes that ridiculed their former masters. Up to 13,000 minstrels take part in this annual festival, which continues to attract large crowds.

Riebeeck's ship. Another day of national remembrance under apartheid was the so-called Day of the Vow or Dingaan's Day (December 16). This commemorated the Voortrekker Andries Pretorius's victory over a Zulu force commanded by King Dingaan in 1838 at the Battle of Blood River. Every year a somber ceremony was observed on this day at the Voortrekker Monument outside Pretoria. Meanwhile, around the country other ceremonies of dedication and church services took place. Since the ending of apartheid, this controversial festival has been renamed the Day of Reconciliation and is a public holiday for everyone to enjoy.

The Day of Reconciliation in South Africa is now an occasion for all peoples to celebrate their identity. Here, Zulu warriors dance at Blood River.

The coastal city of Durban in South Africa's KwaZulu-Natal Province plays host to the annual Beach Africa Festival. Here, sand sculptor Simphiwe Ndlovu shows off his animal sculptures in 2004.

boycotted the event and protested the glorified image of the white conqueror. These groups also organized alternative parades in the weeks that followed.

Festivals and ceremonies have the capacity to either create or diffuse tension. Whatever their form, they are dynamic ways for people to express themselves.

SEE ALSO: Afrikaners; "Cape Coloured" People/Cape Malays; Music and musical instruments; Oral literature; San; Xhosa; Zulu.

FESTIVALS OF PROTEST AND EDUCATION

A number of other festivals are held to raise awareness, stimulate debate, and even to protest against ceremonies being held by other groups. For example, in response to the South African Nationalist government's celebration of the 300-year anniversary of Jan van Riebeeck's landing at the Cape, several organizations joined forces to organize a Defiance Campaign. They

FESTIVAL SONS DA ESCRITA

On November 4–6, 2004 the British Council of Mozambique, in association with the Mozambican organization Acoopal Artes e Letras, held an arts festival called *Festival Sons da Escrita* with the theme "AIDS Can Kill Art." Its purpose was to raise awareness about the impact that HIV/AIDS has had on the lives of millions of people. Local poets and writers gave talks, as well as organizations such as the French medical aid charity Médecins Sans Frontières (Doctors Without Borders). Individual musicians and bands from Mozambique, South Africa, and Brazil performed and ran musical workshops. Movies were screened showing the daily difficulties that are faced by HIV/AIDS sufferers. These events sparked lively debates about how artists might best challenge the misconceptions and stigmas that surround the disease.

HERERO

FACT FILE

Population	150,000 Namibia, 20,000 Botswana
Religion	Christianity; Herero religion
Language	Herero is a term used to include a number of pastoralist groups that speak related languages: Himba, Herero, Tijimba, and Mbanderu. These are all Southwestern Bantu languages related to those spoken by the Owambo people of Namibia.

TIMELINE

1500s–1700s   Ancestors of Herero groups are resident in North and West Namibia.

1840s–1880s   Clashes with Nama, a Khoikhoi subgroup.

1884   German occupation of South West Africa.

1904   Defeat of the Herero rebellion at Waterberg results in the genocide of as many as 65,000 Herero people.

1905   German authorities confiscate all grazing areas that once belonged to the Herero. Many Herero have to work for Europeans on newly established farms.

1915   During World War I South Africa takes control of South West Africa and after the war is granted a mandate to control the country.

1920   Herero forced to live in "homelands," or reserves.

1960   Formation of South West Africa People's Organization (SWAPO), calling for independence from South Africa.

1966   U.N. terminates South African mandate in Namibia. SWAPO begins guerrilla war against occupation forces.

1990   Namibia established as an independent state following the first fully democratic elections.

2004   Germany offers official apology on the 100th anniversary of Herero genocide.

THE BANTU-SPEAKING HERERO OF SOUTHWESTERN AFRICA WERE HISTORICALLY LIVESTOCK HERDERS. MOST HERERO LIVE IN NAMIBIA, THOUGH THERE ARE ALSO SMALL COMMUNITIES IN BOTSWANA AND ANGOLA. THE HERERO WERE THE VICTIMS OF A MASSACRE BY GERMAN SETTLERS IN THE EARLY 20TH CENTURY.

HISTORY

Little is known for sure about the origins of the Herero. Some scholars believe that Herero ancestors arrived in southwestern Africa as early as the fifth century C.E., while others think that they only migrated south from the Great Rift Valley of East Africa in the 1500s. They were certainly well established in the region by the 1700s, with trade links to Portugal's colony of Angola. In the mid-19th century Herero groups clashed with Nama groups who were expanding northward. In 1884, forces of the German Empire began to occupy South West Africa, and in 1904 the Herero rose up against them. By August of that year, the Herero had been defeated, and the survivors driven into the waterless Kalahari Desert to die. Although some Herero managed to cross into Botswana, there were few survivors of this ordeal. The commander of the German forces then issued a notorious "extermination order" to kill any Herero—man, woman, or child— found on "German land."

After South Africa was granted control of the region following Germany's defeat in World War I (1914–18), the Herero were forced to settle in an unviable "homeland."

SOCIETY AND DAILY LIFE

In common with the Himba (see box feature), the Herero were originally nomadic pastoralists who moved with their herds on a seasonal basis. However, they increasingly came to lead a settled life as livestock ranchers on Namibia's central grasslands. Cattle were central to their existence, not only providing food in the form of milk, butter, and meat, but also forming the basis of the economy as walking stores of wealth.

Although this pastoralist way of life is still followed in some areas (for example around Okakarara near the Waterberg in northern Namibia), lack of farmland and overgrazing has forced most Herero to seek other livelihoods. As in other countries in the region (e.g., Zimbabwe, South Africa) reparation for colonial injustices is a crucial question in Namibia, and many Herero look forward to their lands being returned to them.

CULTURE AND RELIGION

In traditional Herero culture, no individuals may own cattle. People belong to groups called *eanda*, which are related through the mother's line of descent. When a boy wants to get married and needs cattle to exchange for his bride, he will not ask his father, who belongs to a different *eanda*, but his mother's brother for the animals. However, the Herero are unusual in having a dual descent system, and so also belong to an *oruzo*, which is a group related through the father's line of descent. After marriage, a boy will live with his father's group and engage in religious practice through his *oruzo*.

Most Herero people have converted to Christianity. The Herero religion, as still practiced by the Himba, focusses on a holy ritual fire (the *okuruo*) that must be kept burning in every settlement by the oldest male member of the *oruzo*. Sacrificial offerings to the male ancestors are made at this fire, which links the living and the dead and also forms the centerpiece of all key events such as name giving, initiation ceremonies, marriages, and funerals.

Many Herero women have a distinctive appearance; they wear an elaborate form of

THE HIMBA

The Himba live in the remote Kunene (Kaokoland) region of northwestern Namibia, where they follow a seminomadic, pastoralist way of life, moving home throughout the year to find suitable grazing land for their animals. They were displaced from their original homeland farther south by Nama raiders in the 1850s, and fled north, where they were dubbed *ovahimba*, meaning "beggars." Many returned to Kunene after the World War I, after Germany had lost control of the territory. Many Himba dress in goatskin loincloths and skirts, wear iron and shell jewelry, and the women cover their bodies in a mixture of ocher, ash, and butter to give their skin a smooth appearance.

European 19th-century dress, with many heavy petticoats, which was introduced to them by German Lutheran missionaries. The link with their herds is recalled in the women's wide "horned" headdresses, which are said to resemble the horns of cattle.

Most Hereros have found ways of combining a modern way of life with their traditional values. In 1955 the Oruano, a Herero church, was founded, which joined Christianity with Herero practices concerning the importance of ancestors.

SEE ALSO: Afrikaners; English-speaking Southern Africans; Khoikhoi; Owambo; Xhosa.

Herero women in their distinctive headgear and clothing. Their full-length, long-sleeved dresses were introduced by German missionaries to replace the Hereros' original "immodest" leather loincloths.

INDIAN SOUTH AFRICANS

FACT FILE

Population	1,200,000 in South Africa
Religion	Hindu (70%), Islam (20%), Christianity (10%)
Languages	English, Afrikaans, Zulu, Telugu, Tamil, and Gujarati.

TIMELINE

1860 The first of 152,000 laborers arrive in Natal from India to work on sugar plantations, roads, and railroads.

1894 Mohandas Gandhi forms the Natal Indian Congress.

1906 Popular resistance to the compulsory registration of Indian people in Transvaal.

1948 National Party comes to power.

1949 Indian–Zulu riots take place in Durban.

1950 Group Areas Act begins forcible removal of Indians living in "white" areas to designated townships.

1953 Reservation of Separate Amenities Act bans Indians and other nonwhite South Africans from using the same public facilities as whites.

1955 Congress Alliance adopts the Freedom Charter.

1964 Indian leader Ahmed Kathrada is sentenced to life imprisonment at the harsh penal facility of Robben Island off Cape Town.

1983 Constitutional reform brings a separate, but subordinate, House of Delegates created specially for South African Indians.

1994 In South Africa's first fully democratic elections, many Indians vote for the Democratic Alliance or the New National Party.

BROUGHT TO SOUTH AFRICA AS CHEAP LABOR BY THE BRITISH, INDIANS SOON SETTLED AND PROSPERED THERE. THEY WERE AT THE FOREFRONT OF RESISTANCE TO APARTHEID, AND NOW FORM AN INTEGRAL PART OF THE DIVERSE COMMUNITY OF THE NEW "RAINBOW NATION."

HISTORY

Most Indians in South Africa trace their origins back to indentured (contracted) laborers transported by the British in the 19th century to work in the sugarcane plantations around Durban and elsewhere in the Natal colony. There, they suffered terrible working conditions and racial discrimination. Yet even though the Indians were expected to return home at the end of their contracts, almost all chose to stay in South Africa, quickly occupying key roles in agriculture, manufacturing, and service industries.

A far smaller group is descended from traders—mainly from Gujarat in western India—who migrated at their own expense at around the same time as the contracted laborers. These incomers typically set themselves up in small businesses. Later, small numbers of Indians left South Africa to settle in other parts of the region.

After the racist National Party's 1948 election victory and the introduction of apartheid, Indians found themselves legally disadvantaged because of their color. In the 1950s, many were forced to move into Indian townships such as Chatsworth in Natal. Along with their housing, education provision was also inferior to that of white South Africans, with a separate Indian higher education facility, the University of Durban Westville (now part of the University of KwaZulu-Natal) being created in the 1970s.

Growing numbers of Indian South Africans joined resistance and trade union movements. The Natal and Transvaal Indian Congresses formed part of the wider antiapartheid coalition led by the African National Congress (ANC). The most famous Indian political activist of this period, Ahmed Kathrada, was found guilty of conspiracy along with ANC leader Nelson Mandela and others in the Rivonia Trial of 1963. Indian resistance to racial oppression in South Africa was pioneered by the renowned civil rights leader Mohandas (Mahatma) Gandhi (see box feature).

A dancer performs a classical Indian routine during celebrations in Durban in KwaZulu-Natal Province in 2001 to mark 140 years of Indian settlement there.

To try to "divide and rule" non-whites by gaining the support of Indian and Coloured People, the National Party reformed South Africa's constitution in the early 1980s to allow both these groups limited access to government. The newly created Indian assembly, the House of Delegates, was allowed to legislate on some aspects of political and social life (including education) but received only limited popular support.

SOCIETY AND DAILY LIFE

Today, many of southern Africa's Indian population work as traders and business people. Most continue to live and work in Durban and other parts of KwaZulu-Natal but are no longer restricted to the Indian townships. Smaller groups live in the greater Johannesburg area and other urban centers.

Indian South Africans have greatly enriched the diverse cuisine of South Africa. Biriyani (rice mixed with meat, raisins, and vegetables and garnished with yogurt) is served on leaves from the banana tree on special occasions. One of the community's signature dishes is Bunny Chow, a quarter of a loaf of bread hollowed out and filled with curried beans, chicken, or lamb.

CULTURE AND RELIGION

Most Indian South Africans are either Hindus or Muslims. While some still speak Indian languages such as Telugu, Tamil, and Gujarati (all protected by South Africa's new constitution), most younger people speak English as a first language, using Afrikaans or Zulu as a second language depending on where they live.

Indian weddings and feasts are colorful occasions. It is common to see Hindu festivals and ceremonies on the beach front at Durban, while the Indian market in that city is a major tourist attraction.

MAHATMA GANDHI

Born in Gujarat, India, in 1869, Gandhi came to South Africa in 1893 to work as an attorney. Appalled by his personal experience of racial discrimination (he was forced out of a first-class train compartment because of his color), he quickly emerged as a leader of the struggle for Indian political rights in Natal. After the British annexed the Transvaal in 1900, he spread his campaign there, developing techniques of peaceful civil disobedience (*satyagraha*) that he was later to apply with great effectiveness in the fight for Indian national independence. Gandhi returned to India for good in 1914, but he remains a hero to Indian South Africans.

SEE ALSO: *Afrikaners; English-speaking Southern Africans; Xhosa; Zulu.*

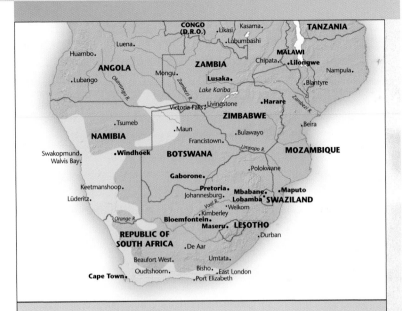

FACT FILE

Population	**South Africa:** 300,000 Griqua, 60,000 Nama, 15,000 Korana, **Namibia:** 100,000 Damara, 80,000 Nama 40,000, Rehoboth Basters, **Botswana:** 1,000 Nama
Religion	Christianity
Language	Afrikaans and Nama, a Khoisan language containing many click sounds. Damara and Korana, spoken by groups of the same names, are "click" languages related to Nama.

TIMELINE

1659–77	Khoikhoi attempt to expel the Dutch from the Cape.
1710	Birth of Griqua chief Adam Kok, founder of Griqualand West.
1713	Smallpox epidemic in the Cape kills many Khoikhoi.
1795	Cornelis Kok I succeeds his father Adam as Griqua chief.
1820s	Arrival of Afrikaner trekkers in Griqualand West.
1840s–1880s	Nama wars against the Herero in Namibia.
1861	Adam Kok III leads trek to establish Griqualand East, encouraged by his British allies.
1870	"Basters" settle at Rehoboth in Namibia.
1879	Griqualand East incorporated into the Cape Colony.
1904	Nama under Hendrik Witbooi fight alongside Herero against the Germans in Namibia.
1920	Establishment of the Griqua Church of South Africa.
1979	"Baster Gebiet" (semiautonomous homeland) established around Rehoboth.
1990	"Baster Gebiet" absorbed into independent Namibia.
2004	Griqua successful in land claims in South Africa's Western Cape Province.

T HE KHOIKHOI WERE, ALONG WITH THE SAN, THE EARLIEST KNOWN INHABITANTS OF SOUTHERN AFRICA. BOTH THE KHOIKHOI AND EUROPEANS ARE ANCESTORS OF THE CAPE COLOURED POPULATION; HOWEVER, OTHER GROUPS OF SUCH MIXED HERITAGE SOON LEFT THE CAPE AND ESTABLISHED INDEPENDENT COMMUNITIES.

HISTORY

When the Dutch arrived in the Cape in 1652, the main people they encountered called themselves the Khoikhoi, or "men of men." These nomadic people formed a number of clans (large groups that share a common ancestor) and spoke a language that could be understood as far as northern Botswana. In the early years of Dutch settlement they were the main source of the livestock needed to provision the ships that stopped at the Cape on their voyage east. The Khoikhoi and the European settlers, among whom there were very few women, soon produced new generations of mixed-heritage speakers of Cape Dutch (Afrikaans), the common tongue of the new colony.

Many of these mixed Khoikhoi–European people decided to leave the Cape Colony, crossing the frontier to assert their independence from Dutch rule. The Griqua, one such Afrikaans-speaking group who originally proudly called themselves Basters ("bastards"), quit the Cape in the 1700s with guns and horses. They were persuaded by missionaries to change their name to Griqua in 1813 in recognition of their strong links with the Grigriqua Khoikhoi clan.

During the apartheid period in South Africa these groups were classified as "Coloured," but since 1994 many groups have chosen to stress their Khoikhoi ancestry. While many Khoikhoi descendants now speak Afrikaans, some 240,000 people in Namibia and South Africa's Northern Cape Province speak Nama, a Khoikhoi language.

Today Namibia, Botswana, and South Africa all have Griqua National Councils that promote a positive Griqua ethnic identity and protect their land and heritage.

SOCIETY AND DAILY LIFE

At the time of first European contact, the Khoikhoi were cattle and sheep herders, but also foraged and hunted for food. They were very mobile and used a series of different grazing areas on an annual cycle. The typical Khoikhoi house was made by women from mats hung over a wooden framework, enabling it be rolled up and transported on the back of an ox. This *matjieshuis*, as it is known, is ideal for the climate, since it allows air to circulate when hot, but swells when it rains, keeping the inside dry. Houses of this kind are still found in a number of communities across southern Africa.

Although some Khoikhoi people still raise livestock of their own, many others have been absorbed into the rural economy as wage laborers on commercial farms.

CULTURE AND RELIGION

Early Dutch settlers told of a long history of strong Khoikhoi male leaders, whose authority was respected by other clan members. This tradition was upheld by key figures in southern African history, such as Adam Kok III (1811–75), the Griqua chief who opposed Boer incursions, and Hendrik Witbooi (1835–1905), a Khoikhoi leader who resisted German forces in Namibia. Passing on names from one generation to the next is a feature of Khoikhoi culture that has survived in some areas despite the widespread use of Afrikaans; interestingly, the same names recur in some of the main families.

Most people of Khoikhoi descent are now strongly Christian, but many stories are told that hark back to pre-Christian times and older beliefs.

See also: Afrikaners; "Cape Coloured" People/Cape Malays; English-speaking Southern Africans.

THE "HOTTENTOT VENUS"

Since colonialism began, Europeans were in the habit of bringing back individuals from distant lands to their home countries. Such people were often shamefully exploited as celebrity attractions, in the manner of a "freak show." In the early 1800s, a Khoikhoi woman called Saarti (or Sara) Baartman became famous as the so-called "Hottentot Venus." Exhibited from 1810 in Britain and then in France, she died in 1816. Her remains were displayed at the Musée de l'Homme, Paris, until as recently as 30 years ago. After apartheid came to an end, a successful public campaign was waged to restore her body to South Africa, and she was buried in 2002 at her birthplace in Eastern Cape Province. Saarti is remembered as an example of the racist demeaning of black Africans by many Europeans during the colonial era. Her life is the subject of an award-winning film by Zola Maseko, *The Life and Times of Sara Baartman*, and a sculpture by the Cape artist Willie Bester.

Khoikhoi dancers honor Saarti Baartman as she is laid to rest in August 2002. Paraded around Europe in the 1810s as an example of curvaceous, "exotic" womanhood, she was used to promote a racist stereotype of Africans.

MARRIAGE AND THE FAMILY

	Birth rate/ 1,000 population*	Infant mortality: Deaths/1,000 births*	Children born/woman Fertility rate: (2005 est.)	Living with HIV/ AIDS in 2003 (est.)	Deaths from HIV/ AIDS in 2003 (est.)
Botswana	23	55	2.9	35,000	33,000
Lesotho	27	84	3.3	320,000	29,000
Madagascar	42	71	5.7	140,000	7,500
Mozambique	36	131	4.7	1.3 m	110,000
Namibia	25	49	3.2	210,000	16,000
South Africa	18	62	2.2	5.3 m	37,000
Swaziland	28	69	3.7	220,000	17,000
Zimbabwe	30	68	3.5	1.8 m	170,000

* per annum (2005 estimate)

The bride and groom at a Hindu wedding in Durban, KwaZulu-Natal Province, South Africa. Under the impact of Western culture, many Indian South Africans have abandoned the practice of arranged marriages.

THERE ARE MANY DIFFERENT PATTERNS OF MARRIAGE AND FAMILY ORGANIZATION IN SOUTHERN AFRICA. MANY BANTU-SPEAKING AFRICANS STILL OBSERVE THE TRADITIONS OF THEIR PEOPLES. IN CONTRAST, FOR THOSE OF EUROPEAN AND KHOIKHOI DESCENT, MARRIAGE AND FAMILY LIFE ARE GENERALLY ARRANGED ACCORDING TO THE CHRISTIAN MODEL.

AFRICAN MODES OF MARRIAGE

Except in the far north of the region, the Bantu-speaking peoples of southern Africa are all patrilineal—that is, they trace descent through the father. As a result, marriage involves the groom's family paying bridewealth (a gift to the family of the bride, often referred to by the Zulu term, lobola). This is not done in order to "buy" a wife, but rather secures the children of the marriage for the groom's lineage. In most societies bridewealth is paid in cattle, although iron hoes (historically, the key agricultural implement for the Shona) once played an important role in Shona marriage arrangements. Today, money or other goods may be substituted in part. Typically in the more influential and wealthy sections of society, some men may have more than one wife. Different societies also vary in the matter of whom a person is permitted to marry: Zulu and Xhosa, for example, cannot marry someone from the clan that they and their mother belong to. Sotho and Tswana, however, are encouraged to marry their cousins, a practice that ensures bridewealth stays within the wider family.

In South Africa under apartheid—the racist system of "separate development" of peoples that lasted from 1948 to 1990—traditional African forms of marriage did

The Zulu religion is still widely practiced. Princess Nombuso Zulu, daughter of King Zwelethini Goodwill ka Bhekezulu, celebrated her royal wedding in traditional style in 2005.

before. The significance of the extended family also began to weaken, while the spread of Christianity brought a decline in polygamous marriage. Today, the AIDS epidemic is bringing about further changes, producing an ever-growing number of orphans and families in which grandparents, rather than parents, play the principal role in raising children.

THE IMPACT OF RACIAL SEGREGATION

During the apartheid period the National Party government criminalized marriage and sexual relations between members of the different legally defined racial groups. These Mixed Marriages and Immorality Acts were among the first laws to be abolished when racial segregation began to be dismantled, in Namibia in 1977 and in South Africa in 1985. Today, a small but growing number of people marry and raise families across former racial boundaries.

SEE ALSO: Christianity; Festival and ceremony.

not have the same legal rights as Western forms of marriage. This inequality exposed women to exploitation by their husbands and their husbands' families. Since 2000, this situation has changed dramatically: African customary forms of marriage now have the same legal standing as civil, Christian, or other religious weddings, if both parties consent to the marriage. Women also now have an equal legal status to men within such marriages, including on matters of property ownership. This is not yet the case in all the other countries of the region.

CHANGING PATTERNS

During the 20th century the growth in migrant labor plus the steady population drift away from the land and toward the cities had a great impact on African patterns of family life. Many households, especially in rural areas, now had a woman rather than a man at their head. The average age at which people got married increased, and they enjoyed greater sexual freedom than

GAY RIGHTS

Homosexuality has not generally been accepted by any sector of southern Africa's population, and gay and lesbian people still suffer much discrimination. Their persecution by President Robert Mugabe of Zimbabwe is an extreme example of the intolerant attitudes gay people face. In stark contrast, South Africa's postapartheid constitution made it the first country in the world—not just Africa—to make discrimination on grounds of sexual orientation unconstitutional. One result has been that partners in same-sex unions now have the same legal protection as married men and women. Compared with the rest of the region, gays and lesbians are also more open about their sexuality in South Africa. However, many devout Christians and traditionally minded members of the African population, who share a conservative moral outlook, still find homosexual lifestyles deeply offensive.

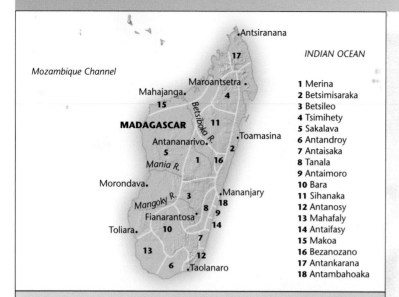

	1 Merina
	2 Betsimisaraka
	3 Betsileo
	4 Tsimihety
	5 Sakalava
	6 Antandroy
	7 Antaisaka
	8 Tanala
	9 Antaimoro
	10 Bara
	11 Sihanaka
	12 Antanosy
	13 Mahafaly
	14 Antaifasy
	15 Makoa
	16 Bezanozano
	17 Antankarana
	18 Antambahoaka

FACT FILE

Population	4,500,000 of a total of 17,000,000 for Madagascar as a whole
Religion	Preexisting religions; Christianity; Islam
Language	Despite being divided into many ethnically distinct groups, all Malagasy speak the Malagasy language. This belongs to the same Austronesian language family as Indonesian and Polynesian, making it the most widely distributed on the planet before 1500 C.E. Because of Madagascar's colonial past, French is also an official language.

TIMELINE

300 B.C.E.	Likely first date of human settlement of Madagascar.
900–1500 C.E.	Many Malagasy communities trade with Africa, China, and the Middle East.
1783–1810	Reign of King Andrianampoinimerina, founder of the Merina kingdom.
1810–28	King Radama I welcomes Christian missionaries and abolishes the slave trade.
1885	France establishes a protectorate over Madagascar.
1896	France overthrows Queen Ranavalona III and annexes the island.
1916	Merina secret society is established to end French rule.
1947–48	France brutally suppresses a major uprising.
1960	Madagascar becomes independent.
1975	New constitution; President Ratsiraka seizes power.
1993	After popular protests and economic liberalization, multiparty politics are restored.
2001–02	Crisis as President Ratsiraka refuses to accept defeat in elections. He finally concedes to the winner Marc Ravalomanana, who becomes president.

THE MERINA ARE THE MAIN ETHNIC GROUP ON THE LARGE ISLAND OF MADAGASCAR OFF SOUTHERN AFRICA'S EAST COAST. LIKE OTHER MALAGASY (PEOPLES OF MADAGASCAR), THEIR ORIGINS CAN BE TRACED BACK TO THE FIRST SETTLEMENT OF THIS PREVIOUSLY UNINHABITED ISLAND FROM INDONESIA IN THE LAST FEW CENTURIES B.C.E.

HISTORY

In addition to the main influx of settlers from Indonesia, similarities of language and culture show that some settlers also came from eastern Africa, though the scale of this migration is unclear. Occupying the central highlands of Madagascar, the Merina took little part in the trans-Indian Ocean trade in which other Malagasy participated during the medieval period. However, from 1780 they established a powerful kingdom that quickly took control of the whole island, helped by European-introduced firearms and ideas of government learned from Europe. In 1896 the Merina kingdom was conquered by France; Madagascar was only to regain its independence in 1960.

SOCIETY AND DAILY LIFE

Traditional Malagasy society is strongly hierarchical, with kinship groups ranked as inferior or superior to one another. This reflects the belief that ancestors are the source of *hasina* (life-giving power), which is unequally distributed between individuals and family groups. Because rulers and nobles had more *hasina*, their descendants had a superior status. These distinctions, and the traditional division of Merina society into nobles, commoners, and slaves, remain powerful even today. The Merina trace

descent through both their father and their mother, but this system is not universal in Madagascar. For example, the pastoral Bara and the Tsimihety, who are chiefly crop growers but also place great cultural and sentimental value on their cattle herds, put a much greater stress on patrilineal inheritance (that is, from the father's side of the family).

CULTURE AND RELIGION

Throughout Madagascar people have a strong sense of the close relationship between their physical and social place in the world and their attitudes toward the dead. People define themselves socially by where their ancestors lived and believe they should return to that area to be buried, regardless of where they may have lived. This holds true for all classes of Merina society, from nobles to commoners. However, people with slaves as ancestors had no ancestral land and so were traditionally deprived of a place in society. Tombs, generally made of stone, are therefore also of great significance to the living. Elaborate rituals are performed there, including digging up the bodies of ancestors, wrapping their remains in new burial cloths and providing new grave goods. These practices continue even though some 40

percent of Malagasy today are Christians. There is also a small Muslim minority, reflecting Madagascar's long-standing trading links with Islamic centers in East Africa and the Middle East.

Diviners and astrologers play a major role in Merina life, identifying favorable days for key activities, such as funerals, weddings, and housebuilding. Since the various points of the compass are associated with different qualities, buildings—and the activities that take place in them—are also organized according to a complex belief system.

See also: Sculpture; Textiles.

Among Madagascar's many ethnic groups, it is not only the Merina who place great significance on burial rites and ancestors. Carved and painted wooden memorial posts known as **aloalos** *and horns of the zebu (a type of cattle) mark the graves of the Mahafaly people from the south of the island.*

FADY—TABOOS ON MADAGASCAR

Like other Malagasy people, the Merina observe *fady*, or taboos, against using certain substances (such as foods) or performing certain acts. *Fady* still govern many aspects of daily life on Madagascar—for example by prohibiting people from denying hospitality to strangers and also making it taboo to refuse such hospitality. Dietary prohibitions vary widely across the island, and even within the same ethnic group, so travelers who want to know how to behave appropriately in different areas must make themselves familiar with a whole range of local customs. One important ecological consequence of *fady* is that many help conserve Madagascar's unique wildlife, including its many species of lemurs, by making it taboo to eat them or to destroy their habitats.

METAL ORES, PRESENT IN ABUNDANCE THROUGHOUT SOUTHERN AFRICA, HAVE BEEN SMELTED AND WORKED THERE FOR ABOUT THE LAST 1,500 YEARS. MINING FOR METALS IN THE REGION IS NOW A MULTI-BILLION-DOLLAR INDUSTRY. THERE IS ALSO A LONG TRADITION OF MAKING METALWORK ART OBJECTS FROM RECYCLED TRADE GOODS.

HISTORY

Incoming Bantu-speaking groups, who migrated into southern Africa from around 300 C.E., brought with them the knowledge of how to smelt iron and copper ores. Metal was clearly so important to these groups that in some places they built their villages with the furnaces at the center. They produced both objects for practical use, such as arrowheads or axes, as well as items for personal decoration, such as jewelry.

In the Late Iron Age metal smelting became such an important activity that furnaces were sited in the bush far away from villages. Metalworking has long been associated with power, since it not only enables a people to trade profitably, but also to make weapons. Thus, ancient kingdoms such as Great Zimbabwe kept firm control over the mining and manufacture of metals, as did the Zulu king Shaka during the Mfecane/Difaqane in the early 19th century.

EUROPEAN INFLUENCES

The arrival of Europeans greatly disrupted many of the existing power structures in southern Africa. The industrialization of manufacturing processes in Europe meant that metals could be worked cheaply and easily, with Africa providing a ready outlet for these goods. Traders flooded the market

THE TREE OF LIFE

In 1995 a project called Transforming Arms into Tools began in Mozambique, sponsored by the International Action Network on Small Arms (IANSA) and the charity Christian Aid. Its aim was to encourage people to hand in weapons left over from the 16-year civil war, which ended in 1992, in exchange for useful equipment such as bicycles and sewing machines. To promote this initiative, four Mozambican artists—Adelino, Fiel, Hilario Nhatugueja, and Cristovao Canhavato ("Kester")—welded a sculpture they entitled *The Tree of Life* (above) from decommissioned pistols and Russian Kalashnikov assault rifles. The finished work stands 10 feet (3 m) high and weighs half a ton; it was exhibited first in Maputo's Peace Park before going on show for five years at the British Museum in London.

and within a few decades in the late 19th century, metal smelting became a rare activity for Africans. People were much more likely to make objects from metal recycled from fencing wire or railroad bolts.

At around the same time, white-owned mining concerns began operations in southern Africa, making it into a key area for the supply of metals, especially gold, to the world. Metal extraction there is still controlled to a large extent by major foreign corporations, such as Anglo-American.

METALWORK TODAY

Most craft metalwork made in southern Africa today uses recycled materials, easily obtainable across the region. Some objects, such as San arrowheads and the Shona ceremonial ax (*gano*) and knife (*bakatwa*), take a traditional form but are made from recycled metal.

Popular art forms from the townships are now made for the tourist trade. These include sculptural figures made from bent wire, often in the form of automobiles or airplanes, but sometimes taking more elaborate forms, such as lizards and chickens. Colorful Zulu baskets using traditional weaving techniques are now created from insulated telephone wire.

The Cape artist Willie Bester (b.1956) has won international fame for his recycled metal sculptures. His work offers a sharp comment on colonialism. For example, *Head North* (1995) shows a metal ox (the iconic beast of burden used by the Boers) with a machine-gun mounted on its back. This powerful symbol of European oppression leaves barbed wire behind it as it marches across the continent.

In KwaZulu-Natal province, a women's craft collective makes objects for sale to the tourist market from telephone wire and beadwork. The craft of weaving recycled wire into baskets began as a pastime among Zulu night watchmen in urban areas.

SEE ALSO: Contemporary art; Shona; Zulu.

SOUTHERN AFRICAN MOVIES AND MOVIEMAKERS

Title	Date	Director	Country
Boesman and Lena	1973	Ross Devenish	South Africa
Izaho Lokanga Ianao Valiha	1978	Raymond Rajaonarivelo	Madagascar
The Gods Must be Crazy	1980	Jamie Uys	Botswana
Maids and Madams	1985	Mira Hameresh	South Africa
Place of Weeping	1986	Darrell James Roodt	South Africa
Mapantsula	1988	Thomas Mogotlane and Oliver Schmitz	South Africa
Sarafina!	1992	Darrell James Roodt	South Africa
Neria	1992	Goodwin Mawuru	Zimbabwe
Fogota	1992	João Ribeiro	Mozambique
Jit	1993	Michael Raeburn	Zimbabwe
More Time	1993	Isaac Mabhikwa	Zimbabwe
Everyone's Child	1995	Tsitsi Dangarembga	Zimbabwe
The Naming	1997	Cecil Moller	Namibia
Night Stop	2002	Lizinia Azueda	Mozambique
Yesterday	2004	Darrell James Roodt	South Africa
Zulu Love Letter	2005	Ramadan Suleyman	South Africa

O NCE SUBJECT TO STRICT CENSORSHIP BY SOUTH AFRICA'S APARTHEID REGIME AND OTHER OPPRESSIVE COLONIAL GOVERNMENTS, MOVIES IN SOUTHERN AFRICA HAVE CHANGED RADICALLY IN MORE RECENT TIMES. NOW, A CONFIDENT MOVIE INDUSTRY IS EMERGING THAT IS NOT AFRAID TO TAKE RISKS AND TACKLE CONTROVERSIAL TOPICS.

MOVIES AND POLITICAL ACTIVISM

In South Africa under apartheid, movies that criticized the Nationalist government not only ran the strong risk of being banned, but could also see their makers arrested, prosecuted, and jailed. The 1988 film *Mapantsula*, directed by Thomas Mogotlane and Oliver Schmitz, was the first film made by black South Africans to tell the story of that community's experience of apartheid. Accompanied by a *pantsula* (township dance) musical score, the picture was shot in the township of Soweto near Johannesburg. It tells the true story of the student riots that broke out there in 1976 and then spread across the country, growing into the first major uprising against apartheid. Because its directors and lead actor (also Mogotlane) were black, and due to its antiestablishment stance, the film was banned in South Africa. In the same year, the well-known South African moviemaker Darrell James Roodt saw his film *The Stick* (about the South African Defence Forces fighting a guerrilla war on the Angolan border) treated in a similar way by the South African censors.

A film crew on a shoot in South Africa. The relaxation of censorship there after apartheid has stimulated new creative energy and talent in the movie industry.

BOOMING MOVIE INDUSTRIES IN SOUTHERN AFRICA

In 1998, Zimbabwe's capital city Harare played host to the third Southern African Film Festival. Its aim was to empower African people through the medium of African film. *More Time*, a movie by the festival's executive director Isaac Mabhikwa showed the dangers of sex in a country rife with AIDS. It delivered a hard-hitting message that was meant to raise awareness about this devastating disease.

Recent movies from southern Africa have been much praised. At the 2005 Berlin Film Festival in Germany, a South African movie, *u-Carmen e-Khayelitsha* (Carmen in Khayelitsha), told the story of the struggles of a local operatic society in the Cape Town township of Khayelitsha to stage Bizet's 19th-century opera *Carmen*. It was awarded the festival's highest award, the Golden Bear, for best picture. At the 2005 Academy Awards in Hollywood, Darrell James Roodt's film about the HIV/AIDS pandemic, *Yesterday*, was nominated in the category of Best Foreign Language Film.

"OUT" IN AFRICA: THE SOUTH AFRICAN GAY AND LESBIAN FILM FESTIVAL

The Gay and Lesbian Film Festival, held in Pietermaritzburg, is an annual celebration of gay pride in South Africa, showing movies that explore and challenge the stigmas attached to homosexuality. The 2005 event began with messages from local celebrities, such as Archbishop Desmond Tutu and comedian Pieter-Dirk Uys. One documentary film shown at the festival—*Clora Venus*, directed by Albert Venter—traced the remarkable transformation of former teacher Rafiq Isaacs into one of South Africa's most glamorous drag divas, Murderess Leoness von Cleef. This film, like many others at the festival, combines humor and tragedy to tell a story that is both intimate and affecting.

EUROPEAN INFLUENCE

The influence of foreign films on the southern African film industry is significant. Foreign moviemakers have also involved themselves in telling southern African stories. In his documentary film *The Swenkas* (2004), Danish director Jeppe Rønde presents a vibrant modern Johannesburg subculture, in which groups of Zulu men dress in their most flamboyant outfits and compete for various prizes.

The 1992 movie Sarafina!, which was based on a hit musical. tells the story of how the school students of Soweto stood up against South Africa's apartheid government. The U.S. actor Whoopi Goldberg played a leading role.

SEE ALSO: *Festival and ceremony; Television and radio.*

MAJOR STYLES AND KEY PERFORMERS

Style	Artist	Country
Bubblegum	Brenda Fassi	South Africa
Chimurenga	Thomas Mapfumo	Zimbabwe
Classical	South African String Quartet	South Africa
Fusion	Johnny Clegg and Savuka	South Africa
Gospel	Rebecca Malope	South Africa
Isicathamiya	Ladysmith Black Mambazo	South Africa
Jazz	Abdullah Ibrahim	South Africa
Jit	Bhundu Boys	Zimbabwe
Kwaito	S'Bu	South Africa
Kwela	Spokes Mashiyane	South Africa
Marrabenta	Fani Pfumo	Mozambique
Mbaqanga	Mahlathini and The Mahotella Queens	South Africa
Reggae	Lucky Dube	South Africa

The Zimbabwean singer Thomas Mapfumo on tour in 2002. A leading supporter of his country's struggle for independence, Mapfumo now campaigns for an end to corruption and human rights abuses in Zimbabwe.

THOMAS MAPFUMO

Thomas Mapfumo, popularly known as the Lion of Zimbabwe, is that country's most famous musician. He started his career in the 1960s playing cover versions of songs by such artists as Otis Redding and Elvis Presley, but began to write his own material in the 1970s. He founded the band Blacks Unlimited in 1978. Singing in Shona, they pioneered a style of music that used the traditional rhythms and melodies of mbira (thumb piano) music (see SHONA). The style became known as *chimurenga* (uprising) music and was strongly associated with the struggle against white rule, which ended with independence in 1980. Since then his songs have remained political with some, such as *Corruption* (1989), directed at the government of his former ally Robert Mugabe. Opposing the Mugabe regime's repression, Thomas Mapfumo now lives in self-imposed exile in the United States.

SOUTHERN AFRICAN MUSIC, A VITAL ELEMENT IN MANY PEOPLES' RITUAL CEREMONIES AND IN RELIGIOUS SERVICES, DISPLAYS A WIDE VARIETY OF STYLES. IN RECENT TIMES, ITS DIVERSITY HAS GROWN STILL FURTHER BY INCORPORATING AND ADAPTING OVERSEAS MUSICAL STYLES.

TRADITIONAL MUSIC

In southern Africa, music was traditionally made for two main reasons: for personal pleasure or for a ceremony. Young boys herding livestock would while away the hours with a reed flute or bone whistle or use horns to signal to one another.

The most basic instrument is the human body, and the music accompanying the San trance dance (see SAN) is created mainly from singing, clapping, and percussion from dance rattles worn around the ankles. These are used by peoples across the region. Another widely used instrument is the musical bow. At its most simple, this is a hunting bow, the sound of which can be resonated with the mouth, or alternatively with a gourd.

Other instruments were traditionally more restricted to a particular area. The thumb piano is mainly found in Zimbabwe (see SHONA), but examples come from elsewhere. Drums were not widely used by Nguni or Khoikhoi groups. Xylophones, which may have originated in Indonesia, are mainly found among the Tsonga, Shona, and Venda, all peoples who historically had contact with the east coast trade.

OVERSEAS INFLUENCES AND LOCAL STYLES

Much musical creativity in recent times has come from local artists reacting to overseas styles. The thriving Cape Town Minstrel festival was originally inspired by a visit by U.S. minstrels in the mid-1800s (see "CAPE COLOURED" PEOPLE). In Mozambique the urban *marrabenta* was played with locally made versions of Western musical instruments. In the 1960s American soul music was also a major influence on local styles such as *mbaqanga*, while Bob Marley's performance in Harare to celebrate Zimbabwean independence in 1980 firmly established reggae as a popular musical idiom throughout the region. During the 1990s, the influence of Hip Hop led to the emergence of the local style, *kwaito*.

A young musician receives instruction in how to play the traditional bow—the player is using his mouth to amplify the sound. His teacher is Pops Mohammed, a South African jazz artist who plays a wide variety of music, from the traditional sounds of the Kalahari to ultra-modern dance styles.

TOWNSHIP MUSIC

The movement of many Africans to towns saw the emergence of music suited to the instruments available. *Marabi*, a home-grown southern African jazz, was played on pianos in the 1920s and jive played on guitars, banjos, and concertinas in the 1930s. In the 1950s pennywhistle jive, also known as *kwela*, became extremely popular (and spread far beyond Africa; the infectious pennywhistle tune "Tom Hark" went to number 2 in the British charts in 1958). More recent artists have also used imported instruments to play locally inspired music such as Thomas Mapfumo (b.1945; see box feature) and his fellow Zimbabwean, Albert Nyathi (see NDEBELE AND MATABELE), who both draw on a range of musical styles.

JAZZ

Out of the *marabi* and swing movements of the 1950s came the phenomenon of African jazz. Dorothy Masuka (b. 1935) and Miriam Makeba (b. 1932) emerged as powerful vocalists, while in the 1960s the trumpet player Hugh Masekela (b.1939) and the pianist Dollar Brand (b.1934; now known by his Muslim name Abdullah Ibrahim) experimented with progressive jazz. Many of these performers left southern Africa during the 1970s and 1980s, and became widely respected in the international jazz scene.

GOSPEL

Missionary and church education has long been a major source of influence on music—in the 1890s the national anthem of South Africa since 1994 "Nkosi Sikelel' iAfrika," was written as a hymn (see XHOSA). Later the Zulu "acapella" style of *isicathamiya* (see ZULU) emerged largely as a way of singing songs of praise. Gospel music is a major part of services of the popular Zionist churches. One of the biggest stars of gospel is Rebecca Malope (b.1970), who launched her career at a talent contest in 1987.

SEE ALSO: *Dance and song; Festival and ceremony; Ndebele and Matabele; Shona.*

NDEBELE AND MATABELE

FACT FILE

Population	1,800,000 Zimbabwe, 700,000 South Africa, 8,000 Botswana
Religion	Christianity, Ndebele religion
Language	Ndebele is an Nguni language, related to Zulu, Xhosa, and Swazi. Northern Ndebele has been influenced by surrounding Sotho–Tswana speakers.

TIMELINE

early 1600s Chief Muzi and followers settle on hills near Tshwane.

1822 Mzilikazi (Khumalo) and his followers quit Zululand.

1870 Lobengula becomes king, with his capital at Bulawayo.

1883 Southern Ndebele conquered by Transvaal Republic.

1888–93 After gaining mining concessions, the British try to annex Lobengula's kingdom. Defeated, he commits suicide and the Matabele kingdom ends.

1896–97 First *chimurenga* (uprising) against white rule in Matabeleland and Mashonaland.

1961 Mainly Matabele Zimbabwe African People's Union (ZAPU) founded to fight white rule.

1965 Unilateral Declaration of Independence by white Rhodesians sparks guerrilla warfare by ZANU and ZAPU.

1980–81 Zimbabwean independence; ZAPU beaten by Robert Mugabe's ZANU in elections.

1981 Homeland of KwaNdebele established in South Africa.

1983 Matabele–Shona conflict. Zimbabwean Army commits atrocities in Matabeleland.

1999 Zimbabwean Movement for Democratic Change (MDC) launched; social problems continue to grow.

THE TERM *NDEBELE* ORIGINALLY DESCRIBED NGUNI-SPEAKING GROUPS WHO MIGRATED INTO INLAND SOUTHERN AFRICA, AN AREA DOMINATED BY SOTHO–TSWANA SPEAKERS. IT WAS LATER APPLIED TO THE FOLLOWERS OF MZILIKAZI, WHO BROKE AWAY FROM SHAKA'S ZULU KINGDOM IN THE 1820S. TODAY THE MAIN GROUP OF NDEBELE PEOPLE, WHO LIVE IN SOUTHERN ZIMBABWE, ARE KNOWN AS THE MATABELE.

HISTORY

Legend has it that, around the early 1600s, Ndebele settlements were established by Chief Muzi on hills near the present-day city of Pretoria. On his death there was a succession dispute between his two sons Manala and Ndzundza, who separated and took their followers north and south respectively to form the two main Ndebele groups. Surrounded by Sotho–Tswana peoples, both these groups—but especially the northern one—have been influenced by their neighbors' language and culture. The Ndzundza were conquered by the Afrikaner Transvaal Republic in 1883 and deprived of their land.

Mzilikazi of the Khumalo clan, one of Zulu king Shaka's generals, left Zululand with his followers in 1822 and settled among the Ndebele near Tshwane. He conquered large parts of the area and absorbed many local people but was driven across the Limpopo River by Afrikaner settlers in 1837. Mzilikazi conquered the Rozwi state in southwestern Zimbabwe and imposed his authority, language, and culture upon it. After his death in 1870 his son Lobengula ruled until Cecil Rhodes' British South Africa Company took control of

A Southern Ndebele (Ndzundza) woman from Middelburg in South Africa's Mpumalanga Province, resplendent in her beaded headdress and neckpiece. The brass necklace she is wearing is also a popular form of adornment among the Ndebele, reserved for special occasions.

Matabeleland, establishing Southern Rhodesia, later called Rhodesia (1965).

After Rhodesia won independence as Zimbabwe in 1980, tensions grew between the Shona—the main ethnic group whose party, Robert Mugabe's Zimbabwe African National Union (ZANU), won the first free elections—and the Zimbabwe African People's Union (ZAPU), founded by the Matabele leader Joshua Nkomo. Massacres occurred in Matabeleland until a truce was signed in 1987 and the two parties merged. In the 2000s, Matabeleland is a stronghold of the Movement for Democratic Change (MDC), which opposes Mugabe's regime.

SOCIETY AND DAILY LIFE

Before the advent of colonialism, the Ndebele and Matabele, like other Nguni speakers, lived by farming and stock

Ndebele women artists are especially renowned for their house-painting skills. The bold, geometric designs on the walls of this church in Mabhoko, South Africa are the work of Francina Ndimande. Another famous mural painter in this tradition is Esther Mahlangu.

NDEBELE HOUSE PAINTING

The brightly painted walls of the homes of the Ndzundza branch of the Ndebele have become world famous. The patterns echo the vividly colored beaded garments and jewelry with which women decorate their bodies. These decorative mural paintings, which are called *kguphu,* draw on a tradition of house decoration taken from the neighboring Pedi people. Originally natural pigments were used, but the availability of modern paints has allowed the full range of bright colors in glass beads to be reproduced on the wall paintings. Together, the striking walls and beadwork can be read as a defiant statement by Ndebele women that, despite losing their land, "We are still here!"

herding. Their staple diet was based around porridge or *iputhi* (today largely made from corn). When the Southern Ndebele (Ndzundza) were overrun by the Boers, their lands were confiscated and they were forced to work on white-owned farms. Despite losing their ancestral lands, they still retained a strong sense of cultural identity.

On conquering the Rozwi state in Zimbabwe, the Matabele imposed a form of rule very like that of Shaka among the Zulu. Men were grouped into age-grade initiation

CULTURE AND RELIGION

The Ndebele religion focused on the *abezimu* or ancestors, who were appeased through sacrifice so that they would look favorably on their descendants. However, the real unifying factor that ensured the wider Ndebele and Matabele nations were held together was initiation (*wela*). It is significant that, within three years of being conquered by the Afrikaners, an initiation school was organized by members of the dispossessed Ndzundza royal family. To this day, the *wela* ceremony, held every four years, remains a very important ritual for the initiation of young men and the preservation of Ndebele identity, and is a source of great pride for the families who take part in it.

The appearance and dress of Ndzundza Ndebele women is also a proud expression of cultural identity. Ndebele women are famous for their brightly colored beadwork. The wearing of beads is governed by a complex set of rules: girls may wear aprons with beaded fringes, but after initiation they must wear the *isiphephetu* (or *pepetu*), a stiff rectangular apron symbolizing that the girl is ready for marriage. In addition, married women are expected to wear some sort of head cover. Today, beadwork is often made and sold as a commercial enterprise.

Beaded aprons and other items are made and worn by Ndebele women to mark the different stages in their progression from girlhood to womanhood. This five-fingered apron is a jocolo, *which is made for a new bride by her mother-in-law.*

SEE ALSO: *Architecture; Contemporary art; English-speaking Southern Africans; Shona.*

groups, which formed the basis of the *impis*, or regiments, that kept order in the state. When Matabeleland was under white rule in the state of (Southern) Rhodesia, the 1930 Land Apportionment Act excluded black ownership of the best farmland. In addition, the levying of taxes forced many Matabele into wage labor in the newly established mines. Since Zimbabwean independence in 1980, the Matabele have suffered as a minority group in a country dominated by the numerically dominant Shona.

IMBONGI—OLD AND NEW

The *imbongi* is a Matabele "praise poet"—an artist who is responsible for celebrating the achievements of leaders and the history of the clan. The *imbongi* would stress the king's positive qualities such as his bravery and skills. Traditional poems record and praise the reign of King Mzilikazi and his son Lobengula. However, in 1999, when the revered Matabele leader and politician Joshua Nkomo died, the dub poet Albert Nyathi was chosen to lead his funeral procession and celebrate his life. Nyathi draws heavily on the culture of the *imbongi*, but accompanies his words both with traditional music and with contemporary blues and jazz. In homage to his praise-poet forebears, his band is called Imbongi.

ORAL LITERATURE

EXAMPLES OF ORAL LITERATURE

The legendary hero **Sororenzou Murenga** of the Shona people of Zimbabwe was renowned for his fighting prowess. He is associated with the first Shona uprising against British rule at the end of the 19th century. Murenga is supposed to have been a huge man, with a head the size of an elephant's, and was inspired by the spirit medium Mbuya Nehanda (see SHONA) to take up arms against the British. He gave his name to the Shona term for the uprising, *Chimurenga*, which means "fighting in the style of Murenga" (i.e. fiercely).

Many **animal legends** are recounted by the San of the Kalahari desert. The San are renowned for their intimate knowledge of the landscape and animals that surround them—a vital survival strategy. One of main figures in their mythology is the predatory insect called the praying mantis, which the San regard as a wily "trickster" figure who can shift shape at will. San herdsmen are reputed to use the "pointing" posture of the insect to discover the whereabouts of lost sheep or goats.

The **creation myth** told by the Zulu centers on a figure known as Unkulunkulu ("ancient one," or "ancestor"). He is said to have grown out of a reed in the mythical swamp of Uthlanga, and proceeded to create everything that exists: mountains, streams, snakes, cattle, and people. Taking the form of a human, he taught the Zulu how to hunt, light fires, and grow crops.

ORAL LITERATURE COVERS A WIDE VARIETY OF LITERARY FORMS THAT ARE PERFORMED OR SPOKEN RATHER THAN WRITTEN DOWN. ORAL LITERATURE IS OFTEN CALLED ORAL HISTORY, SINCE IT CONTAINS INFORMATION ABOUT A SOCIETY'S HISTORY AND CULTURE. IT IS PASSED DOWN BY STORYTELLERS FROM GENERATION TO GENERATION.

EARLY HISTORY

The history of southern African oral literature can be traced to the earliest inhabitants of the region, the San whose inventive and sophisticated folktales, myths, and fables were first recorded by European

NELSON MANDELA'S INAUGURATION

At the inauguration of Nelson Mandela as the first democratically elected president of South Africa in 1994, the traditional role of the praise singer was given new prominence. Zolani Mkiva and Mzwakhe Mbuli, two of South Africa's best known Xhosa praise poets, or *imbongi*, listed Mandela's ancestors, both physical and spiritual, and called on him to lead the new nation. Their dramatic performance celebrated an exciting new phase in southern African history while also stressing the need not to lose sight of the past and its important traditions.

The oral history tradition is alive and well among many African peoples, but nowhere more so than among the San. As young members of his group listen intently, the elder Gaishay Dem of the Ju/'hõansi of northeastern Namibia relates hunting tales.

scholars in the mid-19th century. Since various African animals are central both to the stories and to the rock paintings of the San, there may well be an association between these two art forms.

Through repetition of stories, poems, and sayings, the history, culture, customs and social relations of a people sharing a common language were passed on, and were constantly adapted to the needs of the present. Transmitted from generation to generation, the survival of such stories and legends relied on the memories of each new set of performers. However, greater emphasis was always placed on a storyteller's ability to add new twists to the traditional story than their skill in replicating it exactly.

Another distinctive feature of oral literary forms is that they often called for audience participation. Listeners were encouraged to repeat certain phrases, or to take part in singing or dancing. Audience involvement continues to be a important feature of southern African performance arts today.

PRAISE POETRY

One of the most famous and familiar types of southern African oral literature is praise poetry (see NDEBELE AND MATABELE). The exact nature and purpose of praise poetry varies between different ethnic groups. For example, among the Nguni peoples praise poetry is recited on formal occasions by designated poets and is reserved solely for kings or chiefs. In contrast, among the Shona, the singing of praises is a far less

formal affair, and praise may be addressed to any deserving member of the clan.

Although southern African praise poetry uses certain stock phrases and expressions, each poem is almost always composed spontaneously in response to particular events or occasions. Another interesting facet of this art form is that the performer is not limited to praising his subject. On the contrary, many so-called praise poems are actually critical of the rulers to whom they are addressed, and sometimes even warn them against taking a certain course of action. In such cases, the contemporary praise poet assumes the role of social and political commentator.

ORAL LITERATURE TODAY

Though the introduction of writing and the widespread breakdown of traditional social structures have undermined the importance of oral literatures, oral literary forms do still exist today. In fact, in some instances, the enormous technological advances of the past century and the widening market created by globalization have had a positive impact on oral literary forms, allowing live performances to be recorded and sold worldwide. For example, Gcina Mhlophe, a well-known story-teller, has adapted the folktale tradition for her own television show.

SEE ALSO: *African-language literature; Festival and ceremony; Ndebele and Matabele; San.*

Arts festivals in South Africa often feature poetry performances by local artists and people of the African diaspora. Here, the Caribbean poet Linton Kwesi Johnson recites his work in Johannesburg in 2001.

FACT FILE

Population	900,000 Namibia, 150,000 Angola
Religion	Christianity, Owambo religion
Language	Owambo is a Southwestern Bantu language similar to Herero. The Owambo in Namibia comprise eight groups each with its own dialect: Kwanyama, Ndonga, Kwambi, Ngandjera, Mbalanhu, Kwaluudhi, Eunda, and Nkolomkadhi.

TIMELINE

c.1500	Ancestors of the Owambo settle in north of Namibia along the Okavango and Kunene rivers.
1886	Owamboland brought within German South West Africa.
1919	South Africa given mandate to rule Namibia (South West Africa) by League of Nations.
1949	South Africa grants Namibia's whites the vote. 6,000 farms created for white farmers.
1958	Establishment of Owamboland People's Congress, forerunner of SWAPO.
1966	UN General Assembly votes to terminate South Africa's mandate, though this was ignored.
1968	Owamboland becomes a self-governing territory with its own legislative assembly.
1971	Massive strike of Owambo contract workers, demanding to be sent home.
1970s–80s	SWAPO conducts guerrilla warfare from the north.
1988	Peace settlement sees Cuban troops withdrawn from Angola in return for Namibian independence.
1989–90	UN-supervised elections held in Namibia. First president of independent Namibia is Sam Nujoma.
2005	Second president, Hifikepunye Pohamba, elected.

THE AREA KNOWN AS OWAMBOLAND FORMS A FLOOD PLAIN IN THE FAR NORTH OF NAMIBIA, AND IS THE MOST DENSELY POPULATED AREA OF THAT COUNTRY. AS A RESULT, OWAMBO PEOPLE ARE HIGHLY INFLUENTIAL IN NAMIBIAN LIFE

HISTORY

According to the oral history of their people, which is passed down from generation to generation in stories and legends, the Owambo (or Ovambo) originally came from a region to the northeast, in what is now Angola or Zambia. Their ancestors are believed to have first settled northern Namibia in around 1500 C.E. Owambo history records the existence of several kingdoms by the 17th century.

Germany established a colony in Namibia (then South West Africa) in 1884, but the Owambo were relatively unaffected by this foreign presence until the outbreak of the World War I (1914–18). After South Africa took control of South West Africa in 1919, and later set up apartheid-style "homelands" for the peoples of Namibia, a large part of the Owambo population was forced to work as migrant laborers. As a result, many Owambo became active in the South West Africa People's Organization (SWAPO), fighting for Namibia's independence. The first two Namibian presidents, Sam Nujoma and Hifikepunye Pohamba, both come from Owamboland. The Owambo are by far the largest ethnic group in Namibia, making up around one-half of the total population.

SOCIETY AND DAILY LIFE

Owambo settlements of the past were usually built on raised ground between *oshanas* (shallow drainage channels, or pools). There, people lived through a

A traditional circular, stockaded Owambo village. Dividing the separate compounds are lines of tall poles and vegetation that contain pathways linking the different parts of the village.

combination of cultivating pearl millet (*mahangu*), cattle herding, hunting, and gathering wild foods. Fish were kept in the *oshanas*. Rapid population growth has meant that resources are scarce, so many Owambo now live in more conventional modern homes and work in paid

OWAMBO HOMESTEADS

Historically, the Owambo homestead was a complex arrangement, with a stockade (fence of poles) protecting the people and livestock within from raiders and wild animals. Within this outer fence, separate compounds were created for the male head of the homestead as well as for each of his wives and for the livestock. At the heart of the homestead was a central meeting place where a sacred fire burned. Custom dictated that visitors should announce themselves and wait to be led to this central area. Today, land shortage and the need to find work away from Owamboland prevent many Owambo from living in this way.

An Owambo woman shaping pots in preparation for firing. She is working in the shade of an underground cave so that the clay does not dry out and crack in the intense heat of the sun.

employment, often away from Owamboland. Many Owambo miners have found work in the far south of the country.

Owambo social organization was traditionally matrilineal (based on the female line), and family groups called *omapata* (cooking place) are organized by descent through the mother. Larger clans known as *epata* are believed to descend from the same female ancestor. Inheritance of cattle and other wealth follows the female line, first to a younger brother and then to a sister's son. Increasingly, the pattern is shifting toward a patrilineal society, based on the father's line of descent.

CULTURE AND RELIGION

While the Owambo believe in a supreme creator being called Kalunga, he is seen as a remote deity and is not directly worshipped. The main focus of Owambo religious practices is the ancestors, who are concerned with and involved in human affairs. Neglecting the ancestors may bring

misfortune and illness, and it is the role of the diviner (*onganga*) to identify the offended spirits so that rites may be performed to appease them. Diviners may also specialize in communicating with these spirits, as well as in herbal remedies, breaking the spells of witches, or finding lost items.

Since the Finnish Missionary Society began its work in Owamboland in 1870, Christianity has grown very strong, with most Owambo today belonging to the Lutheran Ovambokavango Church. Some are Roman Catholic or Anglican.

SEE ALSO: Afrikaners; English-speaking Southern Africans; Herero; Khoikhoi.

Owambo "sweepers" at the huge diamond-mining complex at Oranjemund in the far south of Namibia. These workers sweep down to the bedrock in search of gems after giant earthmovers have excavated an area. Despite being so far from home, the miners maintain strong ties to Owamboland.

PORTUGAL'S CONTACT WITH AFRICA BEGAN IN THE FIFTEENTH CENTURY, EARLIER THAN ANY OTHER EUROPEAN NATION. YET PORTUGUESE ("LUSOPHONE") LITERATURE IS THE SMALLEST AND LEAST WELL-KNOWN BODY OF AFRICAN LITERARY WORKS IN A EUROPEAN LANGUAGE.

COLONIAL LITERATURE

Portuguese navigator Vasco da Gama's epic voyage to India around southern Africa in 1497–99 is the subject of one of the great epic poems of the Renaissance, the The Lusiads, by Luís de Camões, first published in 1572. Portuguese colonization of the west coast of Africa had begun as early as 1505. Yet it was only in the late 19th century that southern African Lusophone writing began to emerge. This was due to the low rate of literacy in Portugal's African colonies. The first literary texts by Mozambicans appeared in the *Almanach de Lembranças*, a Portuguese periodical that published work from Portuguese colonies around the world.

In the 1930s, a growing desire for independence in Africa had an impact on the literature of all colonies, including those in Portuguese Africa. From then on, African Lusophone authors looked to the African tradition of oral literature for inspiration.

LIBERATION AND DECOLONIZATION

The wars of liberation in Africa in the 1960s saw writers reject so-called escapist literature in favor of social realism. This was more suited to describing people's social and economic conditions. Writers aimed to encourage an effective liberation movement. Noémia de Sousa (1926–2002), the first female Lusophone poet in Africa, wrote a

1488	Portuguese explorers first visit southern Africa.
1505	First Portuguese trading post established.
1572	Publication of *Os Lusíadas* (The Lusiads).
1885–	Portuguese-language writers emerge in Mozambique.
1961	Establishment of the Front for the Liberation of Mozambique, FRELIMO, which publishes *Poesia de combate* "fighting poetry."
1964	José Craveirinha's poems *Chigubo* and Luís Bernardo Honwana's *Nós Matámos a cäo Tinhoso* (We killed Mangy-Dog).
1975	Portugal grants independence to its colonies in Africa.
1978	Radio dramas based on oral storytelling aired by Belo Marques.
1985	Luis Patraquim: *A inadiável viagem* (The urgent voyage).
1988	Hélder Muteia: *Verdades dos mitos* (Truths of myths).
1989	Eduardo White: *O pais de mim* (The country that comes from me).
1991	José Craveirinha is awarded the Prémio Camões.

collection of angry revolutionary poems entitled *Sangue Negro* (Black blood).

Writers of this period also focused on drama. Strict censorship by the Portuguese authorities tried to stifle critical plays. The colonial regime feared the theater's potential to reach a wide audience, and so the liberation movement encouraged authors to write politically engaged plays.

POSTCOLONIAL LITERATURE

When independence from Portugal was won in 1975, the region's literature again underwent major changes. Authors were freed from the need to champion political causes and so could develop their art in new directions. The trend among Mozambican authors in the postcolonial period, most of whom have focused their energies on poetry, has been to engage with issues of identity, ethnicity, language, and alienation.

SEE ALSO: *African-language literature; English-language literature; Oral literature.*

FACT FILE

Population	49,000 Botswana, 38,000 Namibia, 4,500 South Africa, 1,200 Zimbabwe
Religion	Christianity, San religions
Language	The diverse Khoisan languages split into three main families: southern, central, and northern. Northern Khoisan includes the languages spoken by the Ju/'hõansi, or !Xu. Central Khoisan includes languages spoken by Khoikhoi herders but also some spoken by San such as Nharo, G/wi, and G//ana. Southern Khoisan languages include !Xõ, spoken in southern Botswana, /'Auni-≠Khomani, and /Xam, an extinct San language. The symbols /, //, !, etc. indicate different "click" sounds in these languages.

TIMELINE

c.500 C.E.	Evidence of Bantu-speaking, iron- and pottery-using farmers in the eastern regions of southern Africa.
1652	After Dutch settle the Cape, Europeans begin to spread across southern Africa.
1819–39	The Difaqane/Mfecane (a period of conflicts and mass migrations) causes huge upheaval in the region.
1898	Farmsteads set up at Ghanzi in Botswana's Kalahari.
1961	Central Kalahari Game Reserve (CKGR) established as the San homeland.
1966–67	Botswana gains independence. Namibia–Botswana border fenced, splitting some traditional San lands.
1990	Independence for Namibia sees !Xu and Khwe veterans of the Namibian war resettled in South Africa.
1995	Botswana government forcibly deports San to settlements outside CKGR.
2004	San take the Botswana government to court to protest eviction from their ancestral land in the CKGR.

THE TERM *SAN* WAS ONCE USED BY THE KHOIKHOI OF SOUTH AFRICA'S WESTERN CAPE TO REFER TO PEOPLE WHO DID NOT TEND LIVESTOCK BUT INSTEAD PURSUED A HUNTING AND GATHERING WAY OF LIFE. YET THE SAN PREFER TO SEE THEMSELVES AS MEMBERS OF SMALLER LOCAL GROUPS, OFTEN RELATED THROUGH FAMILY TIES.

HISTORY

It is perhaps partly because of their very local sense of identity that many San groups were readily absorbed by other peoples. At one time San groups lived across the whole range of southern African environments, making their living through hunting and gathering. Things began to change around 2,000 years ago, when the first livestock entered the region and some San groups developed a more settled herding lifestyle.

In eastern areas around 1,500 years ago, different groups of people began to arrive who spoke Bantu languages and who brought with them crops and metals (principally iron) as well as livestock. Many San seem gradually to have been absorbed by these groups, some of whom (for example, the Xhosa and the Zulu) adopted the characteristic "click" sounds of San languages into their own speech. A number of different symbols (such as / and !) are used to indicate these sounds.

First contact was made with European sailors at the end of the 15th century. As Europeans began to settle the coast and the

San hunters in South Africa's Northern Cape Province. The San's nomadic lifestyle has long been under threat from farming and mining concerns, but the land rights of the Ju/'hõansi (in Namibia) and the /'Auni-≠Khomani (in South Africa) were finally recognized in the 1990s.

interior from the 1650s onward, many San had no choice but to work on white-owned farms as their lands were taken over. Those who resisted faced the brunt of Afrikaner aggression, and many San were shot in reprisal attacks for stock theft.

In the 19th century European expansion spread north into Namibia and Botswana, and it was only in the driest areas of the Kalahari Desert, where farming is most impractical, that San peoples managed to maintain an independent way of life until recent times. The loss of land, without which hunting and gathering is impossible, has only gradually been halted.

SOCIETY AND DAILY LIFE

Historically, San people lived by hunting and gathering wild foods in small family-based bands. People took advantage of seasonal periods of plenty to come together with other bands to hold ceremonies and barter goods. The San knew how to adapt their lives closely to their local environment, with the men focusing on hunting while women gathered the majority of food from plants.

Historical evidence from the Cape shows that the San there were very much in tune with their coastal environment, living on food that could be found or hunted along the shoreline. In the very dry areas of the Kalahari, people would move to ensure that they were always near a reliable water source. In other areas like the Drakensberg mountains, people seem to have moved around according to the seasonal migrations of wild animals such as wildebeest.

The establishment of farms and game reserves have disrupted many natural environments, making it increasingly hard to lead a nomadic life. However, hunter-gatherers are seasoned opportunists, and many San people have been quick to identify other new openings as they have come along. For example, many San peoples in Namibia, and to a lesser extent in Botswana, work on large commercial farms. Some have spent time laboring in the mines of South Africa, while others worked for the South African military during the independence war in Namibia. More recently, San people have begun to work as guides for bush tourism, while the women in some remote groups regularly supplement their income by making beaded craft items for sale.

One highly controversial issue is the ongoing struggle between the Botswana government and the San over the right to

OSTRICH-EGGSHELL BEADS

Beads have been made from ostrich eggshells in southern Africa for at least 40,000 years. The process is a laborious one, involving breaking, shaping, stringing, and grinding the shell until perfectly round, shining white beads are produced. These may then be worn on a string as a necklace but are more commonly turned into more elaborate forms of beadwork such as headbands. Historically, beads were given to relatives as a way of confirming friendships, today they are mostly made by San groups in the Kalahari for sale to tourists. The vast number of beads made, as well as the legal protection of wild ostriches, ensures that most of the eggshells are now shipped in from commercial ostrich farms.

(above) A Ju/'hōan hunter from the Kalahari Desert region of Botswana examines ancient rock paintings of hands and animals.

(left) As well as making ostrich eggs into beads, the San would often hollow out and decorate complete shells for use as water flasks or food containers.

impossible for them to stay. In their new homes the San live an unhappy life of dependency as refugees, and are currently mounting a legal challenge to the government's resettlement program.

RELIGION AND CULTURE

There seems to have been a remarkable degree of continuity in San religious practices across very large areas and over long periods of time. Central to this tradition is the "trance dance," which is known from contemporary communities in the Kalahari as well as from prehistoric rock paintings (dating from around 25,000 B.C.E.) and engravings from across southern Africa.

This dance involves all of the community, who come together around a fire to clap and sing. Experienced shamans (healers and mediums between people and the spirit world) become ever more intensely caught up in the dance until they enter into a trancelike state known as *kia*. In this state, a shaman will perform a range of activities, the most common of which involves healing members of the community by laying hands on their bodies to remove invisible "arrows" that are believed to produce illness.

SEE ALSO: Herero; Khoikhoi; Oral literature.

live on ancestral lands in the Kalahari Desert. In 1961, when the country was still a British protectorate, the Central Kalahari Game Reserve (CKGR) was set up as a homeland for the San people, in recognition of the fact that they and their forebears had inhabited this area as hunter-gatherers for almost 30,000 years. In the mid-1990s, the government (pleading economic hardship, but more likely seeking to exploit the Kalahari's potential mineral wealth, especially diamonds and uranium) began moving the San to resettlement camps hundreds of miles away. Their water sources in the Kalahari were removed, making it

LEGACY OF THE /XAM

During the 1870s the German linguist Wilhelm Bleek worked with a number of /Xam speakers from South Africa's Northern Cape who had been sent to prison in Cape Town. This study was continued after his death by his sister-in-law Lucy Lloyd and his daughter Dorothea. It resulted in more than 11,000 pages of text in /Xam with translation. Although this language is no longer spoken in South Africa, this important archive has allowed scholars to reconstruct the language and former lifestyle of the /Xam.

In 2000, South Africa unveiled its new coat of arms. At the base of this is a motto in the /Xam language: "!ke e: /xarra //ke." The punctuation marks signify some of the different click sounds of the /Xam language. The inscription means "diverse people unite," and the fact that it is written in a language that is no longer spoken ensures that it does not favor speakers of any of South Africa's eleven official languages.

MANY SCULPTURES—IN CLAY, STONE, AND WOOD—WERE PRODUCED BY SOUTHERN AFRICAN PEOPLES IN PAST TIMES. THE ANCIENT TRADITION OF CARVING IN SOAPSTONE WAS SUCCESSFULLY REVIVED IN ZIMBABWE IN THE 20TH CENTURY.

EARLY HISTORY

Although representational (lifelike) sculpture is no longer a common practice among the majority of Bantu-speaking peoples of the region, evidence of early indigenous sculpture has been found in many southern African archaeological sites, notably among the ruins of Great Zimbabwe (see SHONA; ARCHITECTURE). Soapstone and clay sculptures from this site, depicting humans and animals, date from between the 13th and 15th centuries.

Other examples of African sculpture are found among the Sakalava and Mahafaly peoples in Madagascar and the Makonde of northern Mozambique. Sculpture in Madagascar dates from at least the 17th century, with both the Sakalava and

A South African sculptor who worked in the European tradition was the Dutch-born Anton van Wouw. This bronze figure is entitled Seated Man with Cooking Pot.

Mahafaly creating large wooden stelae (upright pillars; see MERINA). These stelae, which are known as *aloalos* or *hazomangas*, are carved with different geometrical shapes and human and animal figures, and used to mark burial sites. The Makonde carvings are in ebony wood and depict a variety of human and animal figures. The sculpture of the Makonde is recognized as one of Africa's most sophisticated traditional art forms. Both of these traditions now increasingly supply the tourist market.

EUROPEAN INFLUENCES

Since the arrival of European colonists in southern Africa, sculpture has changed and developed alongside the other visual arts in the region, often in line with global artistic

MAJOR SCULPTORS OF SOUTHERN AFRICA

Sculptor	Country
Anton van Wouw (1862–1945)	South Africa
Edoardo Villa (b.1915)	South Africa
Efiaimbelo (b.1925)	Madagascar
Joram Mariga (1927–2000)	Zimbabwe
Henry Munyaradzi (1931–2002)	Zimbabwe
Lucas Sithole (1931–94)	South Africa
Sydney Kumalo (1935–88)	South Africa
Alberto Chissano (1935–94)	Mozambique
Ezrom Legae (1938–99)	South Africa
Nicholas Mukomberanwa (1940–2003)	Zimbabwe
Sylvester Mubayi (b.1942)	Zimbabwe
Willie Bester (b.1956)	South Africa
Jane Alexander (b.1959)	South Africa

JANE ALEXANDER

One of the most exciting sculptors of recent years is the South African Jane Alexander, winner of the Daimler-Chrysler Award for Sculpture in 2002. Born in 1959, Alexander's talent was evident from early on, and in 1995 her piece *Butcher Boys* was chosen for the Venice Biennale. Alexander produces life-size figures, incorporating animal features, that often have an eerie or menacing quality. She builds the figures up in plaster, and adds found elements like bone or horn. Their disturbing nature has been interpreted as a comment on the mental and physical damage that apartheid inflicted upon South Africa's citizens.

from the 1960s onward. The huge growth in tourism at the end of the 20th century has also had an impact, creating a large market for mass-produced works in traditional styles.

SHONA STONE SCULPTURE

Since the early 1960s a large amount of sculpted work has been produced in Zimbabwe. Mainly sculpted from rocks found in Zimbabwe's Great Dyke, this body of work is referred to as Shona stone sculpture, although the sculptors are by no means all members of the Shona people. Much of the work is in the soft rock called soapstone (or steatite), which can be carved easily. Encouraged by Frank McEwen (1907–94), who set up the Workshop School at the National Gallery of Zimbabwe (then Rhodesia) in the 1950s, Zimbabwean sculptors looked to the traditions of Great Zimbabwe and later carvings, creating works of outstanding skill and beauty. These works have great commercial appeal and there is a large international market for Shona stone sculpture.

trends. Today, professional sculptors in southern Africa work in a wide variety of different media—modeling in clay, carving stone or wood, or creating installations from mixed media and recycled or found objects. Sculpture, as much as the other visual arts in southern Africa, has also changed in response to various social and political pressures, such as the struggles for liberation

The Mahafaly sculptor Efiaimbelo has adapted the traditional grave-post (aloalo) carving of his people to produce modern art. He uses acrylic paints and often incorporates modern themes in his work.

SEE ALSO: *Contemporary art; Merina; Metalwork; Shona.*

FACT FILE

Population	10,000,000 Zimbabwe, 2,500,000 Mozambique, 175,000 Botswana
Religion	Christianity, Shona religion
Language	Several distinct dialects of Shona are now recognized: Korekore (north), Zezuru (midlands), Manyika (east), Ndau (southeast), Karanga (south) and Kalanga (west), as well as Tawara and Tewe in Mozambique.

TIMELINE

200s	Bantu-speaking peoples begin to arrive in southern Africa.
900s	Mapungubwe thrives as a center for trading gold and ivory in the Limpopo valley.
c.1290	Great Zimbabwe rises to prominence, with a population of around 18,000. Smaller similar sites across the region.
1505	Portuguese port established at Sofala to trade with the Mutapa state in the northeast.
early 1600s	The Portuguese invade the Mutapa state.
1889	Cecil Rhodes' British South Africa Company seizes Mashonaland and establishes Southern Rhodesia.
1896–98	First *chimurenga* (uprising) against colonial rule.
1930	Land Apportionment Act bars black people from owning the best farmland in Rhodesia.
1965	Ian Smith proclaims Unilateral Declaration of Independence (UDI); liberation struggle intensifies.
1979–80	Zimbabwe gains independence; first elections won by mainly Shona ZANU under Robert Mugabe.
2002	Mugabe wins fraudulent elections and proceeds with land reform program by seizing white-owned farms.
2005	Mugabe again elected amid violence and vote rigging.

THE CURRENT DISTRIBUTION OF SHONA SPEAKERS ALMOST EXACTLY CORRESPONDS TO THE AREA WHERE ANCIENT STONE-WALLED SETTLEMENTS OCCUR. THE MOST IMPRESSIVE OF THESE IS GREAT ZIMBABWE—CAPITAL OF A THRIVING KINGDOM FROM c.1290–1450, FOR WHICH THE MODERN, SHONA-DOMINATED STATE OF ZIMBABWE IS NAMED.

HISTORY

During the late 1400s, Zimbabwe split into two parts, with the Mutapa state in the northeast and the Torwa state in the southwest. These continued in various forms until the 1830s, when Mutapa was conquered by the Portuguese and Torwa by the invading Matabele under Mzilikazi. Inspired by myths of ancient gold mines, the British South Africa Company took control of the region in 1889. The country was named (Southern) Rhodesia in honor of the British colonial administrator and BSAC founder Cecil Rhodes, and became self-governing in 1923. Resistance to white-minority rule grew after Rhodesia's Unilateral Declaration of Independence (UDI) in 1965, which provoked widespread guerilla war. Following independence in 1980, the country became known as Zimbabwe, but political divisions and conflicts continued through the 1980s between the governing, mainly Shona, Zimbabwe African National Union (ZANU) party and the mainly Matabele-supported Zimbabwe African People's Union (ZAPU) party.

DAILY LIFE AND SOCIETY

Historically, Shona life seems to have focused far less on cattle and other livestock than that of their southern Nguni-speaking and Sotho–Tswana-speaking neighbors. Hoe

agriculture was the basic method of farming and was supplemented by trade. Although Great Zimbabwe and its successor states were characterized by specialization, with certain sectors of the community responsible for mining, metalworking, hunting, and even music, much of this specialization disappeared after the period of mass migrations and wars in the 1820s–30s, triggered by the rise of the Zulu kingdom.

When Southern Rhodesia was established, taxes were imposed and plow agriculture introduced. Taxes could be paid either by working in the newly established mines or by producing food for sale, and both these strategies were employed by Shona people, with some traveling as migrant workers to South Africa to work in the mines there. Some people also labored on the large white-owned commercial farms that were a key

The massive stone walls of Great Zimbabwe, center of a rich Shona state that ruled over a wide area between the Limpopo and Zambezi rivers in the 14th and early 15th centuries.

feature of the Zimbabwean economy until most were forcibly occupied by supporters of Robert Mugabe's ZANU-PF ruling party in the late 1990s and early 2000s.

High levels of education, which is often provided by mission schools, have also equipped many Shona people to take up professional careers. However, the rapid decline of Zimbabwe under the economic mismanagement and corruption of the Mugabe regime has made it very difficult for people to obtain not only luxuries such as petrol but also essential foodstuffs. Withholding food aid has even been used as political weapon. As a result, many educated (and even less well-educated) Shona-speaking people are currently living outside Zimbabwe and sending a portion of their wages back home.

CULTURE AND RELIGION

Shona people recognize a supreme God—known by various names over time but now commonly called Mwari—who provides

rain and speaks through his oracle at a shrine in the Matobo hills. Another important feature of Shona religion is the spirit possession rites or *bira*, which provide an opportunity to communicate with the ancestors (*vadzimu*). At a *bira* ceremony, the mediums, often dressed in black-and-white robes, dance to the music of the mbira *dza vadzimu*, a metal thumb piano (see box feature). Dancing sends the mediums into a trance, and they become possessed by the ancestral spirit, who speaks to the community through them. A number of types of spirit are recognized, the most important

A Shona n'anga, *or diviner. These healers play a key role in the community, using herbal remedies to cure illnesses and helping to diagnose when harmful spirits are at work.*

MBIRA *DZA VADZIMU*

Literally "the mbira of the ancestors," this instrument is a metal thumb piano that provides the music for traditional *bira* ceremonies. It is made of tuned keys of iron mounted onto a wooden board. The board has bottle tops (originally snail shells) attached to it to resonate while the mbira is played. To amplify the sound like the body of an acoustic guitar, mbira are often played in shells made from large hollowed-out gourds, which may nowadays be made of molded fiberglass. Repeating patterns of notes can be played with each thumb, with different total numbers of beats, creating a changing relationship between the musical sequences. The *chimurenga* music of Thomas Mapfumo and others, although played on guitars, is based on the rhythms of mbira playing.

of which are the *mhondoro*—the spirits of ancestral chiefs—each of whom has a dedicated medium and controls a particular area of land as its own spirit province. There is also a belief in evil forces known as *ngozi*, which are thought to be the spirits of murdered people. People call on the services of diviners to identify and ward off the effects of these harmful spirits.

Although Shona people now mostly belong to various Christian churches, many have found ways of combining their Christianity with practices that acknowledge the importance of their ancestors. Services in some independent churches are very similar to the *bira* ceremony but result in possession by the Holy Spirit rather than by ancestors.

SEE ALSO: English-speaking Southern Africans; Music and musical instruments; Oral literature; Ndebele and Matabele.

SPIRITS OF THE *CHIMURENGA*

Mbuya Nehanda and Sekuru Kaguvi were *mhondoro* **spirit mediums who were actively involved in the first** *chimurenga* **(uprising) in 1896, a revolt against colonial rule by the British South Africa Company. They were captured and hanged as ringleaders in 1898, but before she died Mbuya Nehanda declared "my bones will rise again." This was seen as a prophecy of the second** *chimurenga*, **the war of independence fought between 1965 and 1980, when spirit mediums again played an important role in coordinating fighting.**

In 2001–04, severe drought hit southern Africa. Crop failure raised fears of a major famine and aid agencies organized food relief. Among the communities whose land became a dust bowl were the Shona of Kaitano in Zimbabwe's Zambezi Valley.

FACT FILE

Population	Sesotho (Southern Sotho): 3,500,000 South Africa, 1,800,000 Lesotho; Pedi (Northern Sotho): 4,200,000 South Africa
Religion	Christianity, Sotho religion
Language	The Sotho–Tswana are a group of languages within the southeastern Bantu group. These languages are similar but are normally broken into three main groups—Sesotho or Southern Sotho, Sepedi or Northern Sotho, and Setswana in the west.

TIMELINE

c.1300	Sotho–Tswana speaking groups begin to settle in what is now South Africa.
1820s	Moshoeshoe founds mountain kingdom of Basotho (Lesotho) as a refuge from the Zulu Mfecane/Difaqane.
1858–68	Series of conflicts between Moshoeshoe and the Orange Free State; Basutoland loses much farmland.
1870–71	Death of Moshoeshoe; control of Basutoland passes to British Cape Colony, Moshoeshoe's sometime ally.
1910	Basutoland excluded from the new Union of South Africa as a British protectorate.
1966	Lesotho becomes independent.
1972–74	"Homelands" of Lebowa and Qwa Qwa created for the Northern and Southern Sotho in South Africa.
1986	Chief Jonathan, who seized power in Lesotho in 1970, is himself deposed in a military coup.
1994	First fully democratic elections in South Africa and election of the ANC sees the homelands dissolved.
1998	Serious rioting and disorder in Lesotho. Troops from Botswana, South Africa, and Zimbabwe restore order.
2004	Widespread three-year drought across southern Africa brings famine. Lesotho appeals for food aid.

SOTHO-SPEAKING PEOPLES HAVE OCCUPIED THE INLAND PLATEAU REGION OF SOUTHERN AFRICA SINCE AROUND 1300. THEY CAN BE SPLIT INTO TWO MAJOR GROUPS, THE SOUTHERN SOTHO AND THE NORTHERN SOTHO OR PEDI, WHO SPEAK VERY SIMILAR LANGUAGES.

HISTORY

The Northern Sotho are often called Pedi because the Pedi group was dominant from around 1650 onward as a ruling dynasty. This power was disrupted by the Mfecane/ Difaqane (a period of wars and mass migration in the early 19th century), which saw much of the Pedi state collapse under an onslaught by the Matabele led by Mzilikazi in 1826.

At the same time, among the Southern Sotho, the upheaval in the region led to the creation of a centralized state. Moshoeshoe, a chief of the Kwena clan, established a defensive position on a mountaintop at Thaba Bosiu, where he began to take in refugees from the surrounding troubles. By the time of his death in 1870 he had created a nation of 150,000 people, whom he welded together under a single language by placing his relatives as governors among them.

Both the northern and southern Sotho clashed repeatedly with Afrikaner settlers as the latter ventured into the interior, but also with British colonial policy as it sought to intervene. This eventually brought the final destruction of the Pedi state; land was confiscated following the capture of King Sekhukhune in 1879, and Moshoeshoe's southern Sotho nation survived as a British protectorate that eventually became the independent Kingdom of Lesotho.

Though an independent state, Lesotho, surrounded by South Africa, was (and still remains) heavily dependent upon the South

A Basotho man outside a colorfully painted house. He is wearing a characteristic piece of national dress for Lesotho's sometimes cold climate—a warm, woolen blanket.

African economy. Many Sotho men became migrant laborers, working in South Africa's mines and other industries.

SOCIETY AND DAILY LIFE

In the past, most Sotho families lived in compounds made up of linked, circular houses with thatched roofs and straight walls plastered with cow dung. Up until the early 20th century, most people made a living through a combination of crop growing, livestock herding, and gathering wild foods. Cattle formed the backbone of the economy, since they were essential commodities for marriage exchanges. The ideal wife for a Basotho man was the daughter of his mother's brother—in other words, the man whose own marriage had been made possible by the cattle paid as bridewealth for his sister.

THE RAIN QUEEN

The Lobedu people are a Northern Sotho group with traditions that link them with many other southern African peoples. In particular, the royal role of the rain queen Modjadji is common to the Venda and Shona, who also revere sacred monarchy. The Modjadji is removed from the day-to-day existence of her people but dominates their lives like a queen bee at the center of a hive. She has no official husband but is given a coterie of wives by her followers to marry off to form alliances. When the Modjadji is near to death, she commits suicide by drinking poison and is succeeded by one of her daughters. The last Modjadji, crowned in 2003, died in mysterious circumstances in 2005; a successor has not been chosen.

For the initiation ritual marking their passage from childhood to adulthood, Sotho boys and girls wear a reed mask. This young male Lobedu initiate is inside the stockade of the rain queen Modjadji.

The turmoil of the 19th century disrupted much of the established pattern of existence. The Northern Sotho were dispossessed and forced to work on white-owned farms, while the Southern Sotho lost around two-thirds of their agricultural land during Moshoeshoe's conflicts with the Boers. Since large areas of the mountainous Kingdom of Lesotho were too high to cultivate crops, many Sotho-speaking people were forced to look for work elsewhere. As the industrial economy of South Africa developed, migrant labor became a significant part of life for most Basotho and Pedi and remains so today. In the northwest and west of Lesotho, several "camp towns" (for example Leribe, Mafeteng, Teyateyaneng, and the capital, Maseru) grew up as transit points for migrant workers shuttling to and from their employment in South Africa's mines and factories.

Three Basotho riders, sporting the distinctive conical mokorotlo *hat, sit astride their ponies. The Basotho pony, which was bred from horses brought to the Cape by the Dutch, is famous for its stamina and surefootedness.*

CULTURE AND RELIGION

The Sotho religion focuses on the ancestors, and their role as guardians over their descendants. However, Christianity has long been important for the Southern Sotho, and missionaries such as those from the Paris Evangelical Missionary Society, whom Moshoeshoe invited to establish a mission station in 1833, were important advisors in their negotiations with Europeans. Around 80 percent of Lesotho's citizens identify themselves as Christians, with about 50 percent practicing Roman Catholicism.

Rainmaking has long been an important rite for both Northern and Southern Sotho. In the south the indigenous San hunter-gatherers sometimes acted as rainmakers for the Sotho in the past. In the north, an elaborate cult grew up around the Lobedu rain queen Modjadji, who was sent tribute from the surrounding areas (see box feature).

After losing much of their arable land to the Afrikaners, many Southern Sotho were forced to move into the highland territory of Lesotho. This required certain adaptations to the mountainous terrain and extremely cold winter climate. Basotho ponies became an important mode of transport across the rocky mountain valleys.

SEE ALSO: Afrikaners; Christianity; English-speaking Southern Africans; San; Textiles.

THE BASOTHO HAT

A key part of southern Sotho national dress is the Basotho hat or *mokorotlo*. This is made like a cone-shaped basket, woven from grass into complex patterns. The hat recalls the outline of a hill called Qiloane near the fortress built by Moshoeshoe I at Thaba Bosiu. The *mokorotlo* once featured on Lesotho's flag and remains a key symbol of Sotho identity. Today, some Sotho drivers hang a small version of the hat from the rearview mirror of their cars.

SWAZI

FACT FILE

Population	1,200,000 South Africa, 800,000 Swaziland, 1,000 Mozambique
Religion	Christianity, Swazi religion
Language	SiSwati is an Nguni language closely related to Zulu.

TIMELINE

mid-1700s	King Ngwane III leads people inland from the coast to what is now Swaziland.
1820	Chief Sobhuza established capital in the Ezulwini valley where it remains today.
1840–75	King Mswati conquers several surrounding peoples.
1860s	Whites begin to enter territory as hunters, traders, missionaries, and farmers.
1895	Afrikaner South African Republic annexes Swaziland.
1899–1902	In the Second Anglo-Boer War Swaziland becomes a British protectorate at the request of the Swazi queen regent. The period up to independence sees taxes levied and widespread schooling in Christian missions.
1907	British grant the Swazi one-third of their land for their own use. Rights of (white) people holding concessions to the remaining two-thirds are recognized.
1921	King Sobhuza II takes over control from his mother Labotsibeni, who had acted as regent.
1968	Swaziland granted independence from Britain. By this time two-thirds of the land is in Swazi hands.
1973	Constitution suspended by King Sobhuza II.
1982	Sobhuza II, the world's longest-reigning monarch, dies.
1986	King Mswati III ascends the throne.
2004	UN envoy says Swaziland has world's highest rate of HIV infection.

THE SWAZI KINGDOM ONLY DEVELOPED RELATIVELY RECENTLY, IN THE 1840S. TODAY, SWAZILAND IS ONE OF AFRICA'S FEW SURVIVING MONARCHIES AND ITS PEOPLE ARE PROUD OF A HISTORY THAT NEVER SAW THEM CONQUERED IN BATTLE BY EUROPEAN SETTLERS.

HISTORY

The Swazi people have their origin in the expansion during the 19th century of a Nguni state under the leadership of the Dlamini clan. Their name comes from the name of the leader at the time of first European contact, King Mswati, who reigned between 1840 and 1875. The Swazi state fused people from many different traditions and languages into a single nation loyal to the king. Much land was lost when the borders of the country were agreed with Europeans, and many Swazis now live outside Swaziland.

SOCIETY AND DAILY LIFE

Most Swazi live in *imiti*, or homesteads, spread out across the country. People historically lived through a combination of cattle herding and growing corn and millet. Migrant labor in neighboring South Africa has been a fact of life for the last 100 years, and many adult men today spend much of their time away from their villages.

There are more than 70 Swazi clans, and clan membership is passed along the male line with marriage seen as a way of linking clans. Taking more than one wife is acceptable for men in the Swazi tradition, but since each marriage involves giving cattle to the bride's clan, few men are able to afford to marry more than one or two women. Large royal herds allow the King to marry many women; for example, when

Sobhuza II (1899–1982) died, he had 70 wives, giving him connections with clans all over the country. Swazi social organization is dominated and unified through allegiance to the ruling Dlamini clan.

CULTURE AND RELIGION

The Swazi nation is headed by the combined power of the king or *ingwenyama* (lion), and the queen mother or *indlovukati* (she-elephant). Together they hold a balance of power and the system of succession often means that one king will die before his successor comes of age and is able to rule. In such cases the queen mother governs the country as regent until the new king is old enough to take charge.

Swazi religious life is dominated by a concern with the ancestral spirits, or *emadloti*. They can express their anger through illness and misfortune and so must be appeased by the head of the family through gifts of food, meat, and beer. Many Swazi today are devout Christians, but Swazi ceremonial life is still strongly focused on the king and queen mother, who are responsible for the health of the nation, as well as for bringing rain (see box feature).

SEE ALSO: Afrikaners; English-speaking Southern Africans; Xhosa; Zulu.

Women of the Swazi royal family at the umhlanga, or Reed Dance. This annual ceremony involves young girls paying homage to the queen mother by erecting a reed screen around her cattle enclosure.

THE INCWALA CEREMONY

The most important ceremony of the year in Swaziland is the Incwala, and its timing depends on the position of the Sun and the Moon. It is a "first fruits" ceremony, during which the king gives the people permission to eat the new year's produce. Representatives of all parts of Swazi society are required to attend. There are two parts to the Incwala, the first marking the end of the old year, and the second the start of the new year. The king is bathed in the water of all the rivers of the kingdom, as well as the sea, and must "bite" the new crops of the year before dancing in front of his people. Finally, relics of the ceremony are burned in the great cattle pen, after which it is expected that rain will fall.

MAJOR BROADCASTING ORGANIZATIONS

Country	Broadcasters
Botswana	One national television broadcaster, Botswana Television (BTV); one national radio broadcaster, Radio Botswana.
Lesotho	One national television broadcaster, Lesotho Television; one national radio station, Radio Lesotho.
Madagascar	Two national television broadcasters, Télévision Malagasy (TVM) and Madagascar Broadcasting Service (MBS) TV; two national radio broadcasters, Radio Nationale Madagascar (RNM) and MBS.
Mozambique	Two national television broadcasters, Televisão de Mozambique (TVM) and Radio e Televisão Klint (RTK); national radio broadcasters include Radio Mozambique and RTK.
Namibia	One national television broadcaster, Namibian Broadcasting Corporation (NBC) TV; national radio broadcasters include NBC, which runs nine services, as well as Radio Kudu, Radio Energy, Radio Wave and Radio 99.
South Africa	Three national television broadcasters, e.tv, M-Net and SABC, which operates three television channels; the national radio broadcaster is SABC, which operates 19 services, including 5FM, Metro FM and Ukhozi FM.
Swaziland	One national television broadcaster, Swazi TV; the national radio broadcaster is Swaziland Broadcasting and Information Service, which operates three channels.
Zimbabwe	One national television broadcaster, Zimbabwean Broadcasting Corporation (ZBC); one national radio broadcaster, ZBC, which operates four services, Spot FM, Radio Zimbabwe, 3FM, and National FM.

Television is now widespread across southern Africa, bringing news and entertainment to millions of people. Here, a boy adjusts an aerial on the roof of the family home in a South African shantytown.

L ONG SUFFERING UNDER STRICT CONTROL AND CENSORSHIP BY ADMINISTRATIONS OF DIFFERENT POLITICAL PERSUASIONS, RADIO AND TELEVISION IN SOUTHERN AFRICA IS BEGINNING TO GAIN GREATER INDEPENDENCE. HOWEVER, SOME REPRESSIVE GOVERNMENTS, SUCH AS ROBERT MUGABE'S REGIME IN ZIMBABWE, MAINTAIN A FIRM GRIP ON BROADCASTING.

THE FIRST BROADCASTS

Southern African broadcasting began in 1923 with the first wireless broadcast from Johannesburg. The first radio station, JB Calling, was created in 1924, and radio stations in the South African cities of Durban and Cape Town appeared soon after. In the following decade, many other southern African nations followed suit. For example, in 1933 the first Zimbabwean amateur radio broadcast took place and, in the same year, radio broadcasting began in Mozambique.

In 1935, Radio Club de Mozambique founded the LM radio station in the Mozambican capital, Lorenzo Marques (now Maputo).

LM was the first commercial broadcaster in southern Africa, and its programs, consisting of music and entertainment, were mostly presented in English. In South Africa, a 1936 Act of Parliament created the South African

Broadcasting Corporation (SABC), and regulated services began shortly after in both Afrikaans and English. In 1976, SABC launched the first official television service.

STATE CONTROL AND CENSORSHIP

Southern African governments maintained rigid control of broadcasting throughout its early years, and censorship was widespread. In nations ruled by European colonial powers, such as Madagascar and Mozambique, the restrictions on broadcasting and press freedoms became increasingly severe as the independence struggle intensified. These restrictions generally remained in place even after independence, as the new governments attempted to secure their hold on power.

Between 1948 and the early 1990s, the South African apartheid government exercised complete control over broadcasting, not only in South Africa but also in Namibia. This monopoly allowed it to spread propaganda in support of its racist policies and to silence its many critics.

Today, although most national radio and television broadcasting in southern Africa is still state owned, there is generally far more independence and freedom than before. The governments of Zimbabwe and Swaziland, however, continue to restrict the freedom of broadcasters.

THE RISE OF INDEPENDENT BROADCASTING

In 1980, Radio 702, an independent radio station that was highly critical of the apartheid regime, began broadcasting into South Africa from the "homeland" of Bophuthatswana. This marked the beginning of a broader movement in southern Africa away from state-controlled broadcasting and toward independent television and radio stations. In the early 1990s, many southern African states passed laws to reform and liberalize broadcasting. This process was

YFM

The end of apartheid brought seismic changes in South African television and radio. As part of the drive toward independent broadcasting, several SABC radio stations were privatized and new, privately owned radio stations came into being. The most successful of the new ventures has been the radio station YFM. Focused on black youth culture (especially the *kwaito* dance music of the townships; see MUSIC), YFM attracts almost one and a half million listeners weekly. The station produces its own magazine, promotes events, and has its own recording studio. In many ways, this exciting new broadcaster brings together all the positive aspects of the new South Africa, and has become something of a cultural phenomenon. Its loyal listeners identify themselves as the Y Generation.

aided by the creation, in 1992, of the Media Institute of Southern Africa (MISA), a nongovernmental organization with offices in all southern African countries except Madagascar. MISA's aims are to promote diversity, pluralism, self-sufficiency, and independence in southern African broadcasting.

Rude Boy Paul, a presenter on the enormously popular South African radio station YFM, which broadcasts from just outside Johannesburg.

SEE ALSO: *Afrikaners; English-speaking Southern Africans; Xhosa; Zulu.*

CLOTH PRODUCTION IN SOUTHERN AFRICA WAS MOSTLY INTRODUCED BY EUROPEANS, WITH TEXTILES REPLACING SKINS AS THE MAIN MATERIAL FOR CLOTHING. A THRIVING LOCAL INDUSTRY DEVELOPED IN THE 20TH CENTURY BUT HAS RECENTLY BEEN BADLY HIT BY CHEAP IMPORTS FROM INDIA AND THE FAR EAST.

HISTORY

With the notable exception of Madagascar, animal skins were the main form of clothing across southern Africa in precolonial times. Archaeological evidence—in the form of spindle whorls—shows that cloth was being produced at sites such as Mapungubwe (see VENDA) and Great Zimbabwe (see SHONA) by the 13th century C.E. The cotton for this enterprise probably came from India or the coast of East Africa. However, weaving

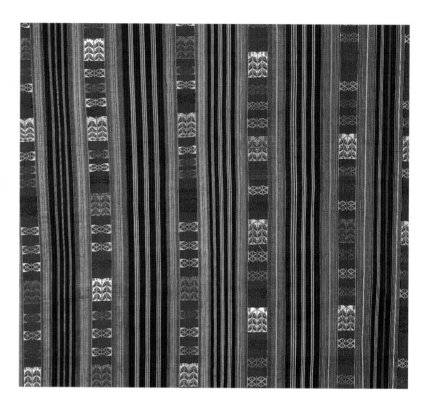

The Merina people of Madagascar used woven silk textiles (lamba) *both as shawls and as shrouds for the dead. Examples of elaborate geometrical designs made for the nobility in the 19th century survive in museums such as the Smithsonian Institution.*

Globalization and southern Africa's textile industry

- A U.S. program, the African Growth and Opportunity Act (AGOA) encouraged foreign investment in Lesotho and Swaziland from Taiwan, Malaysia, and Mauritius in 2000–2003.

- The number of textile workers in Lesotho grew from 20,000 to 55,000 between 2002 and 2004.

- In January 2005, the Multi-Fiber Agreement expired; it was put in place in 1975 by the World Trade Organization to protect against cheap imports by high-volume producers.

- By December 2004, six garment factories in Lesotho had closed with the loss of 6,650 jobs. By July 2005, the number had risen to ten, with 10,000 redundancies.

- As the United States and European Union put restrictions on Chinese textile imports, clothing has been dumped on the African market, causing even more job losses.

- In South Africa, the influx of Chinese, Indian, and Korean clothing cost an estimated 300,000 jobs in 2003–05.

- Average labor costs in the southern African textile industry are $500 per month, but in the Far East just $40–100.

locally produced cotton cloth was labor-intensive and in eastern southern Africa large amounts of cloth—especially colored varieties—continued to be imported, first from India or East Africa and later also from Europe—in exchange for gold, ivory, and other commodities.

In contrast, Madagascar is home to a complex set of weaving traditions. The most elaborate and colorful items produced were the silk shawls (*lamba akotufahana*) made for the Merina aristocracy. After the French conquered the island in 1896 and the Merina monarchy ended, such traditional colored textiles ceased to be made. Recently, however, the tradition has been revived to cater to the tourist and export markets.

A very different material is the bark cloth of Zimbabwe, now manufactured on a commercial scale. Sections of the bark of

A Basotho man wearing a blanket with a poone *(corncob, or "mealie") design, signifying fertility. Blankets form such a central part of life in Lesotho that a saying runs "Bochaba ba Mosotho ke kobo" (The nationality of the Sotho is the blanket).*

trees such as the munhondo or mupfuti are cut away and the tough outer layer removed. The inner core is then softened and stretched into threads that can be used to make cloth for blankets, beer filters, and bags. Such cloth can also be colored using natural pigments and plant juices.

EUROPEAN INFLUENCES

In the 19th century mass-produced, factory-made clothing from Europe steadily replaced skins as common garb across the region. Yet until World War II (1939–45) local industrial output was largely confined to making blankets, rugs, and sheeting. The sector then underwent a period of rapid development, expanding to cover a wide range of synthetic fibers and the manufacture both of garments and of textiles for the home and for industry. This industry was mainly based in KwaZulu-Natal, the Western Cape, the Eastern Cape, and Gauteng.

TEXTILES TODAY

In several areas of southern Africa a modern tapestry industry has developed to supply the export and tourist markets. Tapestry workshops such as those at Teyateyaneng, Lesotho—either private initiatives or sponsored by foreign aid agencies—provide valuable employment, typically for women. But in general southern Africa's clothing industry has been hit hard in the early 21st century by cheap imports from China and India. Thousands of workers have lost their jobs, bringing severe economic hardship to countries such as Lesotho and Swaziland.

SEE ALSO: Merina; Ndebele and Matabele; Shona; Sotho.

BASOTHO BLANKETS

Before the 1860s most Basotho people still wore skins, and blankets were very rare. But by the early 1870s demand for these European-manufactured items had soared and they were being imported from factories in England. Stores were established in many parts of Lesotho to sell them and blankets were—and still are—greatly valued for keeping people warm and dry. Many are decorated with designs that have acquired particular meanings over the years. Basotho blankets are not just worn on special occasions but on a daily basis, for example by mothers carrying babies on their backs. They also feature in important social rituals relating to birth, marriage, and death.

TSONGA

FACT FILE

Population	2,000,000 South Africa, 2,000,000 Mozambique, 250,000 Zimbabwe, 19,000 Swaziland
Religion	Christianity, Tsonga religion
Language	XiTsonga is recognized as an official language of South Africa.

The Tsonga can be split into three main dialect groups, which consist of a number of smaller groups: **Southern:** Maputa, Tembe and Mpfumo—the Ronga groups. **Central:** Khosa, Nkuna, Mavunda, Valoyi, Maluleke, Nhlanganu, and others. **Northern:** Hlengwe, Tswa, and others.

TIMELINE

1500s–1700s	Tsonga kingdoms (Nyaka, Tembe, Maputo) flourish successively in what is now southern Mozambique.
1752	Portugal claims Mozambique as a colony.
1820–21	Invasion of Nguni from Zululand.
1835	Many Tsonga move to South Africa, fleeing Nguni rule.
1858	Death of Shoshangane, leader of the Nguni. Six-year power struggle between rival sons Muzila and Mawewe.
1895	Portuguese war against last Nguni leader Ngungunyane.
1900s	Many Shangaans become migrant laborers in South Africa and Southern Rhodesia.
1962	Frelimo, the Mozambican liberation movement, formed.
1973	Tsonga "homeland" in apartheid South Africa, Gazankulu, declared self-governing.
1975	Portuguese colonialism ends; Marxist People's Republic of Mozambique proclaimed. 17-year civil war begins against South African-backed Renamo guerrillas.
1994	Frelimo wins first free elections in Mozambique; in South Africa, Gazankulu incorporated into the state.

THE TSONGA ARE A DIVERSE GROUP THAT HAVE INHABITED A COASTAL STRIP, NOW MAINLY IN SOUTHERN MOZAMBIQUE, FOR AT LEAST 1,000 YEARS. SEVERAL MAJOR TSONGA KINGDOMS EXISTED BEFORE PORTUGAL COLONIZED MOZAMBIQUE IN 1752. THEREAFTER, THE TSONGA LIVED IN SMALL INDEPENDENT CHIEFDOMS.

HISTORY

In the early 19th century, the Tsonga were affected by the Mfecane/Difaqane (the upheaval caused by the rise of the Zulu kingdom) when an Nguni chief, Shoshangane, fled north into Mozambique after being defeated by Shaka. There he established the Gaza kingdom in 1835, incorporating many Tsonga speakers. Shoshangane's regime created many refugees who fled inland, establishing themselves in South Africa. The alternative name for the Tsonga people, Shangaans, comes from his name.

SOCIETY AND DAILY LIFE

Tsonga peoples value cattle, but their position in a lowland area infested with tsetse fly meant that their economy was more diverse than their Nguni neighbors. Tsonga peoples lived on fish, chickens, and goats, as well as hunted meat. Through their contact with the coast, they were also among the first groups to grow crops introduced from the Americas by the Portuguese, such as cassava, potatoes, and peanuts.

In the 19th century, the Tsonga were active in elephant hunting for the ivory trade, as well as traveling inland to barter cloth and beads for ivory, copper, and salt. Tsonga men have long worked as migrant labor in the mines of southern Africa, where they were commonly known as Shangaans.

CULTURE AND RELIGION

The Tsonga religion recognized a supreme being but focused on the ancestors, who were provided with regular gifts of food and drink. Christianity is widespread among the Tsonga, with worshipers divided among independent churches and the Evangelical Presbyterian Church, formerly the Swiss Mission, which was established there in 1875. When Marxism was imposed in Mozambique by the Frelimo government (1975–88), all religions were banned and their followers persecuted.

SEE ALSO: Afrikaners; English-speaking Southern Africans; Zulu.

TSONGA MUSIC IN SOUTH AFRICA

Tsonga music, from the Mpumalanga and Limpopo provinces bordering Mozambique, has played a key role in the rise of modern South African pop. A pioneer was the singer Francisco Baloyi, whose 1950s recordings were characterized by Latin rhythms (via Portuguese influence) and call-and-response vocals. In the 1970s the Latin element faded and a new style called Tsonga disco emerged, with a male lead singer and a female backing chorus and electric instruments. A later innovation saw Tsonga disco fuse with South African bubblegum pop from the late 1980s onward; Peta Teanet, and Penny Penny exemplified this sound. The track "I Know What I Know" on Paul Simon's *Graceland* album (which introduced South African music to many people in the West) is based on a hit by the popular 1970s Shangaan act General M. D. Shirinda and the Gaza Sisters.

A Shangaan drummer accompanies dancers during a festival at Ulusaba Game Reserve in Mpumalanga Province, South Africa.

FACT FILE

Population	3,500,000 South Africa, 1,250,000 Botswana, 40,000 Zimbabwe, 10,000 Namibia
Religion	Christianity, Tswana religion
Language	The Sotho–Tswana are a group of languages in the southeastern Bantu group. The Tswana peoples are the western peoples of the Sotho–Tswana group and comprise a number of clans that cross the borders between South Africa and Botswana.

TIMELINE

1300s	Tswana settle along the edge of the Kalahari.
1820s	Some 20,000 Afrikaner trekkers cross the Vaal River.
1867	Discovery of diamonds at Kimberley.
1882	Afrikaners invade Tswana lands, subduing Mafikeng.
1885	Tswana ask for British protection; lands south of Molopo River become Crown Colony of Bechuanaland, those to the north the protectorate of British Bechuanaland.
1889	Charter to govern Bechuanaland protectorate granted to Cecil Rhodes of the British South Africa Company.
1895	British government ends BSAC control of protectorate; Bechuanaland Crown Colony annexed to the Cape.
1962	Nationalist leaders Seretse Khama and Ketumile Masire form the Bechuanaland Democratic Party.
1966	Republic of Botswana gains independence.
1967	Diamonds discovered near Orapa.
1977	South African "homeland" of Bophuthatswana granted autonomy; reabsorbed into South Africa in 1994.
1980	Seretse Khama dies; Masire president for next 18 years.
1998	Festus Mogae elected president of Botswana.

T HE TSWANA, THE WESTERN PEOPLES OF THE SOTHO–TSWANA GROUP, ARE MADE UP OF A NUMBER OF CLANS THAT STRADDLE THE BOUNDARIES BETWEEN PRESENT-DAY SOUTH AFRICA AND BOTSWANA. THESE CLANS SPLIT AND RE-FORMED OVER TIME, AS PEOPLE CAME TOGETHER UNDER THE PROTECTION OF POWERFUL CHIEFS.

HISTORY

The Tswana had a certain amount of contact with Khoikhoi pastoralist peoples to the south, such as the Kora and later the Griqua, and were exposed to European technology before encountering Europeans themselves. Tswana lands suffered encroachments from other displaced groups such as Mzilikazi's Matabele as a result of the Mfecane/Difaqane, but also through the arrival of Afrikaner trekkers from the 1820s. The pressure of these settlers on Tswana lands led the Tswana chiefs to seek protection from Britain in 1885.

This boundary that separates Tswana people in South Africa and Botswana is partly the result of the separation of the land north and south of the Molopo River in 1885. The northern areas became a British protectorate, while the southern areas became a British colony, which was later incorporated into the Union of South Africa.

SOCIETY AND DAILY LIFE

Although Tswana people have historically been crop growers and keepers of livestock, the climatic conditions in lands that border the Kalahari Desert mean that drought is a

Tswana girls from the North West Province of South Africa perform a dance on their return from a bojale initiation school.

Tswana baskets from the Okavango region, woven from palm fronds, display great intricacy and variety in their patterning.

constant threat. Sorghum, beans, melons, gourds, and corn can be grown, but Tswana people also supplemented their diet in the past with wild foods. The Tswana's southern Korana neighbors called them the "goat people," suggesting that they once kept large herds of smaller livestock. Cattle herds are still seen as important stores of wealth, necessary for marriage exchanges, but are frequently kept at cattle stations away from the main settlements.

Wage labor became widely established among adult men at a very early stage, with the discovery of diamonds in 1867 at Kimberley, just to the south of the Tswana's ancestral territories. One hundred years later, the discovery of diamonds in independent Botswana greatly boosted that country's

A Batawana fisherman checks his nets on a river in Ngamiland, northern Botswana. The Batawana, a Tswana subgroup, live on the outer fringes of the Okavango Delta, a unique wetland habitat, and play an important part in its conservation.

TSWANA CHIEFS

Before present-day political systems were introduced, leadership among the Tswana depended to a great extent on people's willingness to be ruled. If a chief proved unpopular, people might leave his settlement and place themselves under the protection of another chief. The *kgotla*, or Tswana meeting place, is an important forum for discussion where any tribe member is allowed to express an opinion and be heard by the chief.

In 1895 chiefs Bathoen I of the Ngwaketse, Sebele I of the Kwena, and Khama III of the Ngwato visited Britain, concerned at the way that Cecil Rhodes' British South Africa Company was governing the Bechuanaland protectorate under a charter from the British government. They asked for an audience with Joseph Chamberlain, secretary of state for the colonies. Massive popular support in Britain for the chiefs contributed to the government's decision to end the charter.

The grandson and heir of Chief Khama III, Seretse Khama, visited Britain to study after World War II (1939–45). In 1947 he married an Englishwoman, Ruth Williams, much to the alarm of both Tswana traditionalists and the British colonial government. As a result Seretse was exiled until 1956, when he was allowed to return to Botswana. Seretse Khama became leader of the Botswana Democratic Party and led his people to independence in 1966. His name means "the clay that binds together."

economy. Botswana took 75 percent of profits from the mines; this new prosperity has enabled many Tswana to receive high levels of education and training.

CULTURE AND RELIGION

While recognizing a supreme spirit known as Modimo, Tswana religion, like that of many southern African Bantu-speaking peoples, focuses on the *badimo*, or ancestral spirits. *Badimo* have to be shown attention and respect through regular gifts if they are to look after their descendants. Beyond the household, initiation ceremonies are an important ritual marking the transition into adulthood of both boys (the *bogwera* ceremony) and girls (the *bojale* ceremony).

However, the Tswana were exposed to Christianity at an early stage through the establishment of a mission at Kuruman in 1821. This and other missions were

TSWANA TOWNS

The Tswana are unusual among southern African groups for having long lived in large, concentrated settlements at some distance from their cattle and fields. These settlements were compact, yet could accommodate up to 30,000 people. They comprised individual households, each surrounded by walls forming a *lolwapa*, or courtyard around the house. The houses had straight walls plastered with cow dung and thatched roofs. At the heart of settlement lay the household of the chief; the closeness of a household to the center was an indication of that family's importance within the clan hierarchy.

reasonably successful at converting Tswana leaders, and Christianity has taken firm root among Tswana peoples. Several alternative African and Zionist forms of Christianity have also become well established.

SEE ALSO: Afrikaners; Contemporary art; English-speaking Southern Africans; Khoikhoi.

FACT FILE

Population	1,000,000 South Africa, 85,000 Zimbabwe
Religion	Christianity, Venda religion
Language	Tshivenda is an unusual language that does not belong to either of the major southern African groups—Nguni and Sotho–Tswana. Rather, it has similarities to its northern Shona neighbors with elements from Northern Sotho.

TIMELINE

300s	Soutpansberg area occupied by early Iron Age farming groups.
1220	Mapungubwe kingdom has its center just north of the Soutpansberg.
1300	Decline of Mapungubwe and shift of power north to Great Zimbabwe.
1400	Shona refugees cross the Limpopo River.
1600s	Venda united under Thoho-ya-Ndou.
1760	Capital of Dzata burned down and kingdom divided in two.
1840s	Afrikaners establish province of Soutpansberg on Venda lands.
1872	Christian Berlin Mission established among Venda.
1898	Venda resistance ended by Boer commandos under Piet Joubert.
1973	"Homeland" of Venda declared self-governing.
1979	Venda homeland granted "independence" by South Africa's apartheid government.
1994	Venda reabsorbed into South Africa following first fully democratic elections. Tshivenda declared one of the official languages of South Africa.

THE VENDA LIVE IN THE NORTHEAST OF SOUTH AFRICA JUST SOUTH OF ZIMBABWE. THIS AREA, WHICH IS OCCUPIED BY THE SOUTPANSBERG MOUNTAINS, WAS HOME TO A SUBSTANTIAL URBAN SETTLEMENT AT MAPUNGUBWE MORE THAN 800 YEARS AGO.

HISTORY

The Venda trace their history to a legendary chief, Thoho-ya-Ndou, who united various groups to form the Venda and whose ancestors are said to have come from the Shona areas to the north across the Limpopo River.

SOCIETY AND DAILY LIFE

The main division in Venda society is between the royalty, *vhakololo*, and the commoners, *vhasiwana*. Land is owned by the king and associated royalty, and all commoners are merely tenants on that land. The king avoids all direct contact with commoners, and especially with foreigners.

Venda villages consist of individual households separated by dry stone walls, nestling against cliffs. The king is normally housed at the highest part of the village. The king, who must approach the ancestors on behalf of the nation, is himself treated with the reverence due to a living ancestor.

CULTURE AND RELIGION

The Venda are known for their complex female initiation schools. These are a national event, formed when there are enough girls, and comprise three stages: *vhusha* at puberty, *tshikanda* as a refresher, and *dombani* before marriage. The purpose of these schools is to instruct the girls in what to expect and how to behave as adults, and the teaching is mainly done through dances and songs.

Most rural Venda people live in large farming villages of thatched or stone houses protected by fences or walls and sited on hillsides.

The climax of the *dombani* is the *domba* dance. The women stand in a circle around a sacred fire, each holding the elbows of the initiate in front. They move their arms to the rhythm of a drum, imitating a python, which symbolizes fertility and the motion of a baby in the womb. Many Venda are now Christians, and the attitude of churches toward these ceremonies varies greatly.

SEE ALSO: Afrikaners; Shona.

THE LEMBA

The Lemba are a small group of people who have long lived among the Venda. They used to live by trading and by making metalwork and pottery. The Lemba speak a form of the Shona language called Karanga. They prefer to marry within their own group. The Lemba perform male circumcision and baptism, which the Venda do not, and will not eat pork or any other piglike animals, such as the hippopotamus.

The Lemba refer to local people as *vhasenzi*, a Swahili word used farther up the East African coast to mean pagans. This has led some people to speculate that they may be a remnant of the extensive Swahili trading network that joined the Middle East and the East African coast long before the Portuguese arrived in the 1500s. However, the Lemba themselves have an oral tradition that they are of Jewish origin and migrated to Africa in the fifth century B.C.E.

FACT FILE

Population	7,900,000 South Africa, 20,000 Lesotho
Religion	Christianity, Xhosa religion
Language	IsiXhosa is a Southern Bantu language of the Nguni type. It seems to have been heavily influenced by Khoisan languages since it includes a large number of clicks.

TIMELINE

1780	First Kaffir War with white settlers establishes the Great Fish (Groot Vis) River as a frontier.
1811	British expel Xhosa across the Great Fish River.
1846–47	War of the Ax sees territory between Keiskama and Kei rivers annexed as "British Kaffraria."
1857	A young Xhosa girl, Nongqause, prophesies that if all cattle and crops are destroyed, the whites will be driven into the sea; thousands of Xhosa die.
1865	British Kaffraria becomes part of the Cape Colony
1872–94	The Cape annexes the lands of the Mpondomise, Thembu, and Mpondo.
1910	White-led Union of South Africa formed.
1912	Foundation of the African National Congress (ANC).
1913	Native Land Act limits black people's land ownership.
1948	New Nationalist government introduces apartheid.
1959	Bantustans of the Transkei and Ciskei created for Xhosa speakers.
1961	ANC launches armed resistance
1994	First universal elections; ANC under Nelson Mandela, elected with more than 60 percent of the vote.
1999	Thabo Mbeki elected South African president.

HISTORY

As the first Bantu-speaking peoples to be encountered by Europeans as they spread across southern Africa, the Xhosa speakers have a long history of bitter struggle. The frontier of European control gradually moved across their territory between 1780 and 1894, a period of wars and social upheaval. The most devastating episode for the Xhosa was the self-inflicted "cattle killings," a religiously inspired attempt to rid the land of white settlers. Starvation and death ensued, causing the population to drop from 105,000 to 37,000 between January and July 1857, and 33,000 survivors to migrate to the Cape to seek work on white-owned farms. Christian missions were set up among the Xhosa in the 1820s. The high level of mission education, as well as their history of opposing white rule, saw Xhosa-speaking people feature prominently in the political movements of the 20th century. South Africa's first two presidents, Nelson Mandela (who is of Thembu royal descent) and Thabo Mbeki, are both native Xhosa speakers.

King Xolilizwe Sigcawu of the AmaXhosa subgroup from the Eastern Cape. In 2001, Britain apologized to the king for colonial injustices against the Xhosa. Other main Xhosa subgroups such as the Thembu recognize their own royal clans.

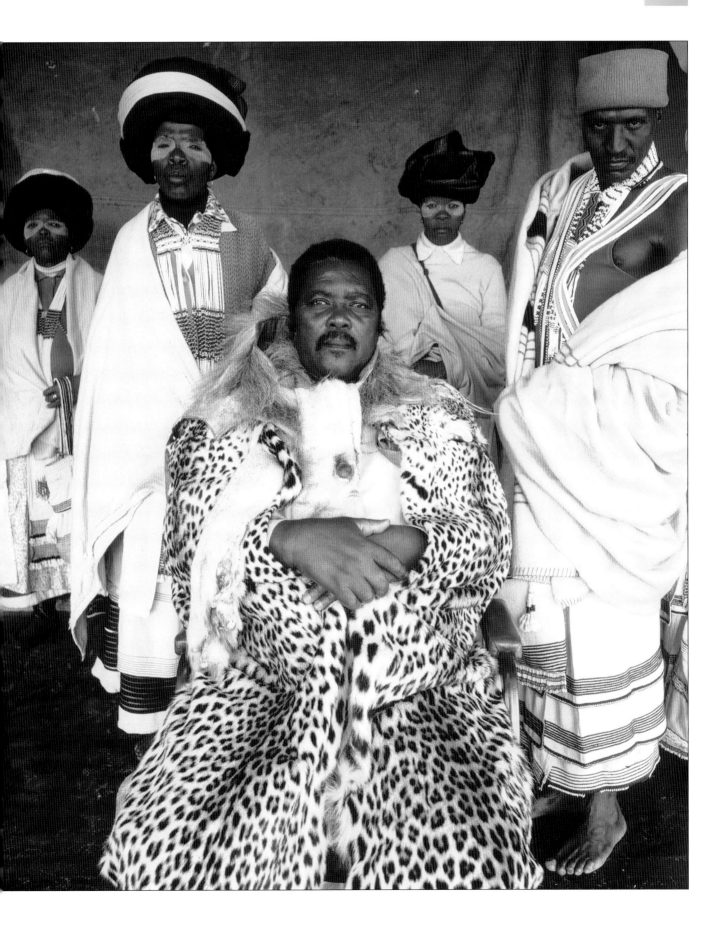

SOCIETY AND DAILY LIFE

Like other Nguni peoples, life historically focused on homesteads of beehive-shaped huts built around a central cattle pen. People lived by herding cattle and sheep and by growing crops such as corn; porridge made from this cereal formed a staple part of their diet. Men looked after the cattle, while boys herded sheep, and women were responsible for growing crops.

From the early 20th century onward, the Xhosa began to make a distinction between the educated urban elite of so-called "School people," and the "Red people," who followed a more traditional way of life. ("Red" refers to the red ocher that rural people used to rub into their skin.) School people were marked out by their Western-style dress and by the shape of their huts, which were square rather than round.

Xhosa male initiates into adulthood (amakwetha) *gather outside a lodge. The young men smear themselves with white clay in preparation for the initiation rite, and during the ceremony itself wear headdresses made of lamb's wool and feathers.*

XHOSA INITIATION

One of the binding forces that has long been used to bring people together in Xhosa society is male initiation. To become respected as an adult man, it is essential to pass through this ritual. The ceremony focuses on a sacred rite of circumcision, after which the boys go into the bush for a period of healing and learning. There they are taught the skills of hunting, but also the correct way to behave, laws of respect, and how to honor the ancestral spirits. The ceremony ends with the *amakwetha* dance, in which the initiates move from homestead to homestead wearing headdresses and with their bodies painted white. After this they are cleansed and anointed with butter while all their possessions are burned. They then return as men to their parents' houses, where they are given presents.

Xhosa women may be recognized by their large woolen "turbans." They are also famous for their colorful beadwork. The beadwork tradition arose in the 19th century when the Xhosa, who then lived on the frontier, acquired many beads from traders and developed some elaborate forms of decoration.

Xhosa-speaking people have worked on white-owned farms since the early 1800s, and in South Africa's coal, diamond, and gold mines since the 1860s. Missionary schools, the most famous of which is Lovedale, have been responsible for educating a long line of Xhosa speakers. One of the first such "School people" was Tiyo Soga (1829–71), who in 1857 was ordained as a minister in Scotland. He later returned to South Africa, where he worked as a missionary, translating the Bible as well as John Bunyan's *Pilgrim's Progress* into Xhosa. Today many educated Xhosa work as teachers, lawyers, and priests.

CULTURE AND RELIGION

Today, most Xhosa speakers are Christians, yet many independent Christian churches incorporate some preexisting beliefs and practices. For example, bridewealth (*lobola*) is still given by Christians.

In common with other Nguni peoples of southern Africa, the original religion of Xhosa speakers focused on the ancestors, who were supposed to watch over the crops and herds. People could communicate with the ancestors not only through sacrifices of cattle and beer but also via diviners, who were distinguished by their white clothing. However, the immense suffering that followed the "cattle killings" caused many Xhosa to lose faith in such worship.

There is a long history of literature in Xhosa. Leading writers of recent times include the novelists Guybon Sinxo (1902–62) and A. C. Jordan (1906–68).

See also: African-language literature; Afrikaners; English-speaking Southern Africans; Sotho; Zulu.

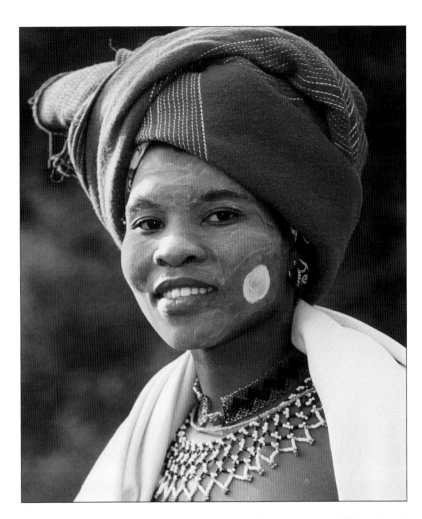

NKOSI SIKELEL' IAFRIKA

The song *Nkosi Sikelel' iAfrika* was composed in 1897 by Enoch Sontonga (c.1873–1905), a Xhosa speaker. He wrote the first verse and chorus in his native language. Sontonga had been educated as a teacher at Lovedale and was working at the time at a Methodist mission school near Johannesburg. In 1925 it was adopted as an anthem by the ANC, and in 1927 seven extra Xhosa stanzas were added by the poet Samuel Mqhayi (1875–1945). In 1994 the hymn became the National Anthem of South Africa. Sontonga's original words run as follows:

Nkosi, sikelel' iAfrika;	*Lord, bless Africa*
Malupakam'upondo lwayo;	*May her spirit rise high up*
Yiva imitandazo yetu	*Hear thou our prayers*
Usisikelele.	*Lord bless us.*
Chorus	*Chorus*
Yihla Moya, Yihla Moya,	*Descend, O Spirit*
Yihla Moya Oyingcwele	*Descend, O Holy Spirit*
	Lord bless us
	Your family.

FACT FILE

Population	10,650,000 South Africa 250,000 Lesotho, 75,000 Swaziland, 2,000 Mozambique
Religion	Christianity, Zulu religion
Language	Zulu is an Nguni language of the southern Bantu group. It is very similar to Swazi and Ndebele and has much in common with Xhosa. Zulu has taken three clicks from the Khoisan languages that preceded it in southern Africa. Zulu is the most widely spoken language in South Africa, and is common in Johannesburg, as well as in KwaZulu-Natal.

TIMELINE

c.1000	Nguni people settle the eastern seaboard between Drakensberg mountains and the sea.
1816	Shaka becomes Zulu leader, sparking the violent upheaval known as the Mfecane/Difaqane (crushing).
1828	At his death, assassinated by his brother Dingaan, Shaka has conquered all the peoples of KwaZulu-Natal.
1835	Afrikaners create Republic of Natalia south of Zululand.
1838	Zulu defeated by the Boers at the Battle of Blood River.
1843	British annex Natalia as the Crown Colony of Natal.
1879	Zulu–British War; British defeated at Isandhlwana, but finally crush Zulu at the Battle of Ulundi.
1906–08	Last Zulu uprising led by Chief Bambatha.
1910	Natal becomes part of the new Union of South Africa.
1959	Apartheid "homeland" of KwaZulu created for the Zulu.
1994	Zulu leader Dr. Mangosuthu Buthelezi, founder of Inkatha Freedom Party (1975) becomes home affairs minister after South Africa's first free elections.
2004	Inkatha wins 38 percent of the vote in KwaZulu-Natal in national elections.

S TRICTLY SPEAKING, THE ZULU ARE JUST ONE CLAN OF THE NORTHERN NGUNI PEOPLES. YET UNDER KING SHAKA THEY GREW INTO A MAJOR POWER IN SOUTHERN AFRICA IN THE EARLY 1800S. THE DYNAMIC NEW NATION HE CREATED ABSORBED MANY CONQUERED PEOPLES, AND THE ZULU ARE NOW THE LARGEST ETHNIC GROUP IN SOUTH AFRICA.

HISTORY

Zulu dominance among the northern Nguni began in the late 1700s, with leaders demanding tributes from neighboring peoples. One reason for the rise of the Zulu may have been their desire to control the ivory trade with Europeans at Delagoa Bay in what is now southern Mozambique. The height of Zulu power came under Shaka, who ruled between 1816 and 1828. His most important innovation was to restructure Zulu society along military lines. Initiation age grades—boys of a similar age initiated into manhood together—were reorganized into the *Amabutho* regiments, which Shaka later deployed with great effectiveness to run his expanded empire. These units employed new military tactics incorporating the use of the *assegai*, a short-handled stabbing spear ideal for hand-to-hand combat, which replaced the earlier throwing spear.

This period of ongoing upheaval and conflict, at the center of which was the Zulu kingdom's military expansion, is known in southern Africa as the Mfecane/Difaqane. The effects of Zulu conquests spread like

Members of the Zulu royal family assemble at the Reed Dance, a ceremony the Zulu share with their neighbors the Swazi. The shields and knobkerries (heavy hardwood clubs) they are carrying recall the strong military traditions of the Zulu since Shaka.

ripples in a pond right across southern Africa, as large numbers of homeless refugees—as well as rebel offshoots from the Zulu kingdom, such as the Matabele and the Ngoni—conquered other parts of the region. The cycle of violence and dispossession went on for 20 years, from 1819 to 1839.

LADYSMITH BLACK MAMBAZO

The world-famous all-male Zulu group Ladysmith Black Mambazo sings *isicathamiya*, an unaccompanied close-harmony vocal style that arose in the mines of South Africa. Migrant workers, far from their homes and families, developed this type of music and then brought it back to Zululand, where regular competitions were organized. The group was founded in 1964 by the singer Joseph Shabalala, who asked his brothers and cousins to join. Its name alludes to their prowess in the singing competitions: the town of Ladysmith in KwaZulu-Natal is where the Shabalala family come from, and "black" refers to black oxen—thought to be the strongest—while "Mambazo" means *ax*, a symbol of the group's ability to cut down their competitors.

SOCIETY AND DAILY LIFE

As other peoples were absorbed into the Zulu kingdom, they were encouraged to adopt a Zulu way of life, inhabiting beehive-shaped huts, raising cattle, and cultivating crops. Women had responsibility for growing sorghum, corn, peanuts and beans, while men looked after the cattle, whose *amasi*, or curdled milk, was a local delicacy. Cattle were chiefly important, however, as vital currency in marriage exchanges, or lobola, by which a male lineage gained not simply a wife from another clan for one of its members, but also the right to any children subsequently born to the wife.

After the British defeat of the Zulu in

Joseph Shabalala of Ladysmith Black Mambazo dances at a Zulu harvest festival. The group have become South Africa's musical ambassadors; in 1993, Nelson Mandela asked them to accompany him to the award of his Nobel Peace prize in Oslo.

The Themablethu craft village in Hluhluwe, KwaZulu-Natal province, is a community-driven project enabling Zulu women to sell their renowned craft items direct to tourists. Here a woman from the collective shows off a beadwork earring.

1879, the community was taxed for the first time, so many Zulu men had to work as migrant laborers in South Africa's mines. Their nation's military past gave them a reputation for strength and bravery, and key roles were reserved for them in the mines.

The warlike history of the Zulu surfaced again in the early 1990s, as the Zulu Inkatha Freedom Party feuded violently with the African National Congress as apartheid came to an end.

CULTURE AND RELIGION

Like their neighbors, the Swazi, the Zulu were formerly unified by the person of the king. The king was at the center of major national rituals such as the first-fruits festival marking the start of a new year. The most sacred royal object is the *ink'atha*—a coil of woven fibers symbolizing the way in which the nation binds together its people. The Inkatha Freedom Party (originally a cultural movement) takes its name from this.

Zulu religion focuses on the ancestors, or *amadlozi*. They are appealed to with gifts to ensure they look favorably on their descendants. *Sangomas* are specialist diviners who are able to interpret the wishes of the *amadlozi*, and can be recognized by their wigs of threaded white beads. A great many Zulu people are now adherents of Christianity, though a number of churches have found ways of incorporating aspects of preexisting practices into Christianity.

Zulu women are well known for the high-quality craft items that they make to sell, in particular beaded items and woven baskets. The weave is so tight that such baskets were even used in the past for storing beer.

SEE ALSO: *Afrikaners; English-speaking Southern Africans; Music and musical instruments; Xhosa.*

THE LANGUAGE OF BEADS

Brightly colored glass beads have been widely used by the Zulu since the 1800s. They are used to create patterned ornaments worn on the body or around the head or waist. Flat panels of patterned beadwork have become famous as Zulu "love letters." These were traditionally made by teenage girls for young men, and the combinations of colors expressed a particular meaning. For instance, white would denote purity and truth, while red could mean passionate love but also anger and pain. The exact interpretation of the message depended on an intimate knowledge of the relationship, so people other than the intended recipient would not be able to "read" these secret love letters.

Any of the words printed in SMALL CAPITAL LETTERS can be looked up in this glossary.

a cappella An unaccompanied form of singing, such as the ISICATHAMIYA singing style developed by the Zulu.

adobe Dried clay or mud, widely used as a building material throughout Africa.

age-grades The different social level in certain societies. Each person is part of an "age-set" (a group of similar-aged peers) who move up as they grow older through the various age-grades, gaining in status.

agriculturalist A settled (sedentary) farmer who makes his or her living by cultivating crops.

aloalo A decorated wooden memorial post put up by the Mahafaly people of Madagascar to mark a grave.

amadlozi The revered ancestors of the Zulu people.

apartheid (Afrikaans: "separateness") The system of ethnic segregation introduced by the Nationalist government of South Africa in 1948. Officially defined as "separate development of the races," apartheid was in fact a tool of oppression designed to shore up white domination.

banning A restriction of freedom used by the APARTHEID regime in South Africa to silence its opponents. Banning orders restricted the movements of a person and prevented her or him from meeting more than one other person at a time.

Berlin Conference on Africa A meeting held in 1884–85 to reduce tension between the European colonial powers by agreeing spheres of influence in Central Africa. It recognized Belgian King Leopold II's claim on the Congo Free State, and granted all countries free access to the Congo and Niger rivers.

bridewealth A common practice among African peoples, in which a marriage is sealed by a gift given by the groom to the family of the bride. This gift is often in the form of cattle, but may also be other livestock or money.

chimurenga (Shona: "uprising") A revolt by the Shona against British colonial rule in 1896. The term came to be applied to the independence struggle to free Rhodesia (Zimbabwe) from white-minority rule in the 1960 and 1970s, and also to the MBIRA-based music created by Thomas Mapfumo in support of the liberation war.

clan A social group made up of several extended families or LINEAGES. Clan members often trace their descent from a common ancestor.

Difaqane A Sotho-Tswana word meaning "scattering." It refers to the period of mass migrations (see MFECANE) caused by the rise of the Zulu kingdom under King Shaka in 1819–28.

divination A feature of many African religions, divination is practiced by ritual specialists, who use a variety of tools to find out the cause of misfortune, accidents, or illness.

eanda A social group among the Herero of Namibia, comprising people related through the mother's line of descent. Other groups based on the father's line of descent are called *oruzo*.

epate A large CLAN among the Owambo people.

fady The term for a TABOO among the Merina people of Madagascar.

groundnut An alternative name for the peanut, which forms the staple diet and major cash crop for many peoples of sub-Saharan Africa.

homeland In APARTHEID South Africa, a region created by the government to accommodate black African peoples. They were often nowhere near peoples' ancestral lands, and had poor land, facilities, and infrastructure. People were forced to live in these homelands (also called Bantustans) after having been evicted from areas designated for "whites only" by the 1950 Group Areas Act.

hominid A member of the family Hominidae, relatively large-brained primates that walked upright on their hind legs (bipedal). Some species of hominids, known as australopithecines, are considered ancestral to humans. Their fossils have been discovered at sites in East and southern Africa, plus one find in Chad.

hunter-gatherers People such as the San of the Kalahari Desert who depend on wild resources for their food. They live by hunting wild animals, fishing, and gathering plant foods and other materials.

indentured laborer A person drafted on a fixed, low-wage contract to work abroad on a specified task or major project. Many Indians, for example, were brought to South Africa by the British colonial authorities to work on sugar-cane plantations in Natal.

infibulation The custom of female circumcision (also called female genital mutilation). It is practiced by some African peoples, and involves sewing up the vulva. It is harmful to a girl's health and is strongly discouraged by health authorities and aid workers. Some countries have outlawed the practice.

imbongi A praise poet among the Matabele, responsible for celebrating the achievements of leaders.

imiti A Swazi homestead.

impi An armed body of men among the Zulu. Impis were formed into effective Amabutho regiments by King Shaka during his reorganization and mobilization of the Zulu nation in the early 19th century. Impis inflicted a major defeat on British forces at the Battle of Isandhlwana in 1879.

Incwala The "first fruits" festival of the Zulu and the Swazi, at which the king is honored and the blessings are asked for by the people from their ancestors.

Isicathamiya An A CAPPELLA singing style that evolved among migrant Zulu workers in hostels in KwaZulu–Natal, eastern South Africa, in the 1920s. Its most famous modern exponents are the group Ladysmith Black Mambazo.

isicathulo The gumboot dance, characterized by rhythmic stomping, created by black South African mineworkers.

kguphu The Ndzundza Ndebele practice of painting decorative and colorful murals on the outside walls of houses.

kraal A group of traditional beehive-shaped homes of the Zulu set in concentric circles around a central cattle enclosure.

lineage An extended family group that shares a common ancestor. If the society traces its origins to a male ancestor and descent is traced from father to son, the lineage is termed patrilineal. If the ancestor is female and descent is traced from mother to daughter, the lineage is matrilineal.

lobola A term used by Bantu-speaking peoples in southern Africa for BRIDEWEALTH.

marabi An early form of jazz played in South Africa from the 1920s onward.

masquerade A festival in which masks and costumes are worn. Many African cultures have elaborate masquerades marking important RITES OF PASSAGE such as initiation.

matjieshuis (Afrikaans: "mat house") A portable house made of mats and a wooden frame and used by the seminomadic Khoikhoi people.

mbaqanga A style of five-part harmony singing that became popular in South Africa in the 1960s.

mbira (thumb piano, lamellaphone, sanza) An instrument widely used in sub-Saharan Africa. It is made of tuned metal strips attached to a resonating chamber (often a hollowed-out gourd). The keys are plucked with the thumbs.

Mfecane (Nguni: "crushing") The term used by the Bantu peoples east of the Drakensberg Mountains to refer to the wars and migrations that affected southern Africa in 1819–39, linked in part to the emergence of the Zulu kingdom.

mhondoro In the Shona belief system, the spirits of influential people who act as intermediaries between people and the creator god Mwari.

mokorotlo The characteristic cone-shaped woven hat worn by Sotho men. It has become a national symbol of the kingdom of Lesotho.

ngozi Harmful ancestral spirits in the Shona religion; they are thought to be the spirits of murdered people.

nomad (adj: nomadic) A person who follows a wandering lifestyle, usually living either by herding livestock or trading. The movements of nomads or seminomadic people, such as the San of the Kalahari, are determined by the need to find new grazing pastures, or by trade demands.

oshana Shallow drainage channels that surrounded the traditional settlements of the Ovambo people of Namibia and Angola. They were used as defensive barriers and as fish ponds.

pantsula A popular and lively style of TOWNSHIP dance in South Africa.

pastoralist A person who lives by herding livestock such as cattle or sheep and generally pursues a nomadic or seminomadic lifestyle.

polygyny The practice of marrying more than one wife.

protectorate A state or territory under the control of a stronger foreign nation. The term was often used by European powers to refer to their African colonies.

reliquary (adj. and noun) A container used to hold the remains of a person, or a term to describe such a vessel.

rite of passage A ceremony, such as initiation into adulthood or marriage, that marks the passage of a person from one stage of life to another.

savanna Tropical grassland dominated by various species of perennial grasses interspersed with shrubs and low trees. Much of tropical Africa is characterized by this terrain.

shantytown An area of impermanent housing, usually made from scrap materials, on the outskirts of large cities where poor migrants to urban areas live. Shanty towns often lack running water, drainage, and other basic amenities.

shebeen An illegal TOWNSHIP bar in South Africa.

shifting cultivation A farming method (once termed "slash-and-burn" agriculture) that involves clearing an area of forest for temporary crop growing. After harvesting the crop, the farmers move on to a new location.

subsistence farming A type of agriculture in which all the crops grown are eaten by the farmer and his family, leaving nothing to sell for profit ("cash crops") at market.

taboo A restriction or prohibition, established by convention in a culture, which prevents a person from acting in ways seen as inappropriate. Many taboos relate to tasks that must not be undertaken by one sex or the other, food that must not be eaten, or certain forms of clothing that may not be worn.

township Government-built SHANTYTOWNS put up in the APARTHEID era in South Africa to house people evicted from "white" towns. Their inhabitants' labor was still needed in the cities, so many township dwellers were bused daily on long journeys to and from their place of work. Townships such as Soweto outside Johannesburg and those on the Cape Flats outside Cape Town became hotbeds of resistance to apartheid.

trekboer (Afrikaans: "migrant farmer") An Afrikaner farmer who settled inland in the 18th and 19th centuries.

tsetse fly An insect that carries parasites that transmit disease to both people and cattle. It is responsible for the spread of sleeping sickness (trypanosomasis).

Umhlanga An annual ceremony performed by unmarried girls to pay homage to the Queen Mother of the Swazi people. A reed screen is erected around the monarch's enclosure, and the ceremony is also known as the "Reed Dance."

urbanization The process by which a rural area becomes more built-up and industrialized. This generally involves the migration of rural people into cities.

Voortrekker (Afrikaans: "pioneer") An Afrikaner who took part in the Great Trek (1836–45), when farmers of Dutch descent left the Cape of Good Hope seeking new lands in the interior after the British authorities at the Cape outlawed the keeping of slaves.

wattle-and-daub A building technique that uses clay or adobe plastered on a latticework made of sticks.

Wela The male initiation ceremony held by the Ndebele.

zimbabwe A house or enclosure constructed by the Shona from the 1200s onward. Settlements of such structures were built by the dry stone wall method (that is, using no mortar).

General books:

Beckwith, C., and Fisher, A. *African Ceremonies* (Harry N. Abrams, Inc., New York, NY, 2002).

Hynson, C. *Exploration of Africa* (Barrons Juveniles, Hauppauge, NY, 1998).

Mitchell, P. J. *African Connections: Archaeological Perspectives on Africa and the Wider World* (AltaMira Press, Walnut Creek, CA, 2005).

Morris, P., Barrett, A., Murray, A., and Smits van Oyen, M. *Wild Africa* (BBC, London, UK, 2001).

Murray, J. *Africa: Cultural Atlas for Young People* (Facts On File, New York, NY, 2003).

Philips, T. (ed.) *Africa: The Art of a Continent* (Prestel, Munich, Germany, 1995).

Rasmussen, R. K. *Modern African Political Leaders* (Facts On File, New York, NY, 1998).

Reader, J. *Africa: A Biography of the Continent* (Penguin, New York, NY, 1998).

Sheehan, S. *Great African Kingdoms* (Raintree/Steck-Vaughn, Austin, TX, 1998).

Stuart, C., and Stuart, T. *Africa—A Natural History* (Swan Hill Press, Shrewsbury, UK, 1995).

Temko, F. *Traditional Crafts from Africa* (Lerner Publishing, Minneapolis, MN, 1996).

The Diagram Group *Encyclopedia of African Peoples* (Facts On File, New York, NY, 2000).

The Diagram Group *Encyclopedia of African Nations and Civilizations* (Facts On File, New York, NY, 2003).

Thomas, V. M. *Lest We Forget: The Passage from Africa to Slavery and Emancipation* (Crown Publishers, New York, NY, 1997).

Books specific to this volume:

Mandela, N. *Long Walk to Freedom* (Back Bay Books, New York, NY, 1995).

McDonough, Y. Z. *Peaceful Protest: The Life of Nelson Mandela* (Walker and Company, New York, NY, 2002).

Mills, G., and Hex, L. *The Complete Book of Southern African Mammals* (Struik, Cape Town, South Africa, 1997).

Nagle, Garrett *Country Studies: South Africa* (Heinemann Library, Oxford, UK, 1999).

Nicholson, R. *The Zulus* (Chelsea House, New York, NY, 1994).

Sheehan, S. *South Africa Since Apartheid* (Hodder Wayland, London, UK, 2002).

The Diagram Group *History of Southern Africa* (Facts On File, New York, NY, 2003).

Thompson, L. *A History of South Africa* (Yale University Press, New Haven, CT, 2001).

Useful Web sites:

www.aids.org.za
South Africa's AIDS Foundation Web site.

www.cheetah.org/?nd=home
Web site of the Cheetah Conservation Fund, saving one of Africa's most endangered species.

www.gov.za
Official Web site of the South African government.

media1.mweb.co.za/mosa
South African museums and heritage online.

www.panda.org.za
World Wide Fund for Nature (WWF) South African branch.

www.peaceparks.org
Transfrontier conservation in southern Africa.

www.sadc.int
Website of the Southern African Development Community.

www.san.org.za
WIMSA (Working Group for Indigenous Minorities of Southern Africa) is an umbrella organization for the region's San peoples.

PICTURE CREDITS